S. Clement Leslie

The Rift in Israel
Religious Authority and Secular Democracy

SCHOCKEN BOOKS · NEW YORK

Published in U.S.A. in 1971
by Schocken Books Inc.
67 Park Avenue
New York, N.Y. 10016

© S. Clement Leslie 1971

Library of Congress Catalog Card No. 76-150986

Printed in Great Britain

The Rift in Israel

Contents

Preface

This book is an essay in interpretation, not a work of scholarship. Its primary material was gathered in about 100 interviews in Israel, from Dan (or a few miles short of it) to Beersheba. This was supported by a programme of reading, whose nature will be clear enough from the text and references.

The question which the book seeks to answer was born in my mind during a first visit to Israel shortly before the Six-Day War. The impulse to investigate was encouraged by the editor of *International Affairs*, and even more by Norman Bentwich who supported and nourished it, as friend and counsellor, without stint of his time, experience and wisdom, during nearly two years.

The first outcome was a pair of articles in *International Affairs* in 1969. Since these aroused some interest, and were reckoned both in Israel and in London to be not too far off target, I went on to extend their scope and deepen their probings. Six or eight short passages from them are included in the present text, which also overlaps a little the material of an address to the Anglo-Israel Association in May 1970.

Almost every one of the many and diverse men and women approached in Israel was generous with time and thought, frank in spirit and clear in exposition. I am sincerely grateful to them all. There are seven to whom I have particular reason for gratitude, since as they well know I made unusual demands on them, all fully met. They are (and I leave the order of the names to the hazard of the alphabet) Joseph Bentwich of Jerusalem, Rabbi Jack J. Cohen of Hillel House, Jerusalem, Dr Harold Fisch, Rector of Bar-Ilan University, Ephraim Kritzler of Kibbutz Lavi in Galilee, Uzi Peled of the Israel Institute of Applied Social Research, Chaim Raphael of London and Sussex University, and Aryeh Simon of Ben Shemen Youth Village.

Finally, there is my wife. I am more grateful to her than I can well say, not only for helpful criticism, but for cheerfully coping over

vii

many months with the impact on her home and her own work of the activities required by an intensive project of this kind.

London, Autumn 1970   S. C. Leslie

Some Hebrew Terms

Aliyah   'Ascent'. Immigration to the Land of Israel.

Diaspora   (Greek). Dispersion: the totality of Jewish communities outside Israel.

Halacha   The 'oral law', originally and accurately so called in distinction from the Hebrew scriptures. Then codified and written down in the earliest centuries AD in the Mishna, later embodied in the Talmud. The meaning of the word itself is close to that of 'The Way' as used in the Gospels and applied by early Christians to their own sect.

Histadrut   Lit. 'organization'. The Israel General Confederation of Labour.

Kibbutz   pl. *Kibbutzim*. Collective settlement.

Kosher   More strictly '*Kasher*'. Conforming to religious dietary laws. So '*Kashrut*', the regime of dietary conformism.

Mitzva(h)   pl. *Mitzvot*, religious rule or obligation.

Moshav   Co-operative settlement, combining private holdings and separate family households with joint planning and marketing.

Sabra   Israel-born. Name of the cactus fruit, 'prickly outside, sweet within'.

Shabbat   Israeli-Hebrew for Sabbath. The Ashkenasi and Yiddish form is Shabbas.

Torah   The Five Books of Moses: alternatively, the Hebrew Scriptures. The word means 'teaching', wrongly rendered in the Greek Septuagint as 'nomos' and so into New Testament English as 'Law' – a cause of much misunderstanding.

Yeshiva   pl. *Yeshivot*, rabbinical academy or school.

Background

I

1800 BC—AD 135

There is a Youth Village within a few miles of the airport of Lod, the Lydda of the Bible, on which the author was privileged to spend a week gathering material for this book. The children at Ben Shemen are mostly of African or Asian descent, picked for brightness. The older ones speak English well – far better than the average teenager in Israel – and were intrigued that a stranger should come to write about their country. A group of them met to ask him why. The first question came from a seventeen-year-old girl, with a sweet and gentle face and sightless eyes. Why should anyone abroad by this time be interested in anything about Israel except that they are good at fighting wars? The children murmured a little: they understood what she meant. They had their own answers but wanted to know the visitor's. So may the prospective reader of this book.

The State of Israel was established as a homeland for the most homeless of peoples and a refuge for the most savagely oppressed. It has turned out also to be the framework within which the immemorial spiritual issues hidden in Judaism can expose themselves and find their latest opportunity for resolution. Because Judaism is part of the foundations of Western civilization, what it can achieve on its first modern appearance in its own secular State must be of profound interest at a moment when those very foundations are being shaken by forces from which Israel herself is not immune. By its very nature, by its intense preoccupation with individual and social conduct, by the spiritual tensions that mark it, Judaism when it is free to express itself is bound to face and wrestle with questions of universal concern. In Israel, it is doing so this day. Now that the Jewish people is once more wielding political responsibility after the normal fashion of the age, it once more finds itself in the forefront of the human adventure. Whether this is by nature or messianic destiny, it is involved beyond hope of evasion in all the main dilemmas of the time: the dilemmas of national interest and universal morality, of power and self-restraint, of communal purpose and individual ambition. Moreover its involvement has a most peculiar character. Its problems are not only everyone's problems in the sense of resembling others', but of actually *being* others'. The involvement is direct.

Take the most obvious instance. Its tiny territory is at the heart and focus of great power confrontation. The fate of superpowers and their satellites may well depend on the way it conducts itself. The ancient prophecy of Armageddon as the final battle scene – the hill of Megiddo, by the historic route to the north from Sinai – could still be borne out. It is a party also to another of the great confrontations, the long-deferred encounter between the West and a resurgent Arab world, whose future role though not yet clear is bound to be fateful. There is yet a third field of potential catastrophe, in which Israel may be called on to play a decisive part: anti-Semitism, the buried dynamite that is still capable of signalizing by its explosive force one more of man's headlong retreats into savagery and war. In this, Israel is involved not only in its own name but through its unique network of linkages with other nations. These linkages, for good or ill, are mediated by the world-wide Jewish communities who look to Israel with a special regard. Jewish minorities live among a variety of peoples who may yet be subjected by history to unforeseeable strains and temptations – stresses in whose outcome Israel's own stature and policies would be sure to play their part.

There are also other problems, domestic in their apparent scope but in fact equally of world-wide concern. The greatest of these is the reconciliation of personal freedom with the central economic authority that modern technology requires: the reconciliation of communal purpose with individual motive. The non-Communist world is grappling with it, not yet with success. It could be a life-or-death matter. Israel has achieved an approach to this which owes much to the traditional teaching of Judaism. But her solution is not final: the most advanced of social democracies, she is changing under influences from within and from the wider world. If she can find new syntheses, new solutions, the world under its own intensifying pressures is bound to take note. Whether she will find them depends on how much fertility and power of growth still resides in the ethic of communal living, the characteristic element that marks out Jewish ethical teaching and thought as unique.

It is here that we touch the nerve of our present argument. What

4

Israel will make of the issues she faces depends on the quality of her people's thinking: her choices must be determined by the spiritual level on which she operates. This in turn depends upon the outcome of an ideological tension, a conflict of ideas, which goes to the root of the State's existence and character. The broadest and deepest moral issues that can be faced by any national state are between the narrower and wider conception of its interest – between its duty to itself and its duty to mankind. In trade and tariffs, in arms supply and aid, in the selection of friends and the acceptance of enmity, in the decision to stand firm, bend or give way, the process of choice never stops for any nation. It is inherent in the fact of nationhood, which in spite of varied religious allegiances is for practical purposes, for life-and-death purposes, man's chief repository of value in this age – his grail or his Moloch. Said Martin Buber, perhaps the nearest thing to a minor prophet that modern Jewry has produced,

> The typical individual of our time is no longer capable of believing
> in God, but he finds it impossible to believe even in his own
> substance – that substance which has neither pediment or basis –
> and so he holds fast to his faith in his expanded ego, his nation, as
> being the highest authority within his reach . . . he transforms his
> nation into an idol, he sets up the personality of his people as God.[1]

But what if nationhood is seen by a people as prescribed by God Himself, as carrying with it an eternal mission, enshrined in a perpetual covenant, not an act of self-worship but a hard external command issued and accepted, not self-deception but an authentic fact, bearing as its warrant the incredible, unanswerable fact of survival? This vision has always been the characteristic mark of the Jewish people. Even for many of those for whom the Exodus story is no longer literal history, who would indeed disavow religious belief, this vision of mission and destiny, of ultimate redemption for man, with the people of Israel both agent and beneficiary, still remains alive. To all such minds the preservation of nationhood is an absolute duty.

There have always been other Jews, who were content with, indeed preferred, a group life, national or parochial, without messianic overtones. Historically – whatever the present-day moral – it was these who were apt to fall away, whom the prophets denounced, whom the Spaniards compelled to forswear their faith, who became Christians when the Enlightenment broke down social barriers. Now, in their own State, they have no great pressures to endure. They are denounced by religious authority, but without the prophetic resonance. For what destiny they have been liberated, what their influence will be, what will become of a state in which they loom large, are questions as yet not answerable, which we shall examine. There are faint signs of quite new possibilities.

For our immediate purpose, the significant points are two. One is that it is this strange compound of opposed attitudes and philosophies of life that has shaped and will shape the policies of the State, with their fateful implications for the rest of the world. The other point is at a deeper level than policy-making. The real, the determinant problems being worked out in Israel are spiritual. Within its borders an established faith that rests its claims wholly upon historic revelation fights to maintain itself against the two disparate forces that threaten it. On the one hand is the secular spirit of the age, weighed down under the burden of its man-made values, blindly adrift on an unknown sea. On the other is an increasingly wide spread and urgent search, on the part of men and women some religious, some secular, for the inward vitality of faith and for some objective measure of its discovery. These are the conflicting forces it is our purpose to describe.

Before we embark on their closer examination it seems necessary to provide an outline of the background to these contemporary issues in the character of traditional Judaism. Those with some knowledge of Jewish history and tradition may pass it over, unless perhaps they wish to sharpen their teeth on its rough material, or are curious to know how this very old story, so encrusted with memories for them, has struck the untutored eye of a latecomer. For other readers – and this is its purpose – it may render more meaningful some of the stranger features of the life of the mind in the Jewish republic.

The Being who first broke in upon the dark consciousness of the pagan world did not – according to the Pentateuchal record – expound Himself as idea: He made demands, He issued orders, He demonstrated power, He required obedience. This remains the basic character of Jewish monotheism.

It is fundamental, too, that the original vision was a historical event – a revelation made through a man to a people at a point in time. For that people Sinai was history, an early and crucial stage in the great cosmic drama in which their God had cast them for the central role. A historical drama must have a central figure: if it is to have universal meaning, and to be played out through centuries on the stage of history, the figure cannot be an individual – it must be a people. And that people must be given a part to play – a task to perform, a rule to obey (obedience being both the task itself and the guide to its performance) and a promise to inspire it. Here then are the essential ideas – the designation of a people (Election), the assignment of a mission (to fulfil the Law, as witness), the imposition of a rule (the Torah, the code for living) and the Covenant in which the Almighty offers and the people accept the promise of fulfilment.

In a famous medieval religious tract called the *Kuzari*, the poet-philosopher Jehuda Halevi puts incomparably the Judaic conception of the identity of revelation and history. The book is in form a dialogue between a Rabbi and an eastern ruler who in the end is converted to Judaism – an event with a firm basis of fact in the eighth-century history of the Crimea. The Rabbi is asked to explain his belief:

'I believe in the God of Abraham, Isaac and Israel, who led the children of Israel out of Egypt with signs and miracles; . . . who sent Moses with His law, and subsequently thousands of prophets . . . Our belief is comprised in the Torah – a very large domain.'

Al Khazar (the Ruler): . . . 'Now shouldst thou, O Jew, not have said that thou believed in the Creator of the world, its Governor and Guide, and in Him who created and keeps thee . . .?'

Rabbi: 'That which thou dost express is religion based on speculation and system, the research of thought, but open to many doubts.' (Then he explains that the only way to describe God is by his deeds.) '. . . God commenced His speech to the assembled people of Israel: "I am the God whom you worship, who has led you out of the land of Egypt," but He did not say: "I am the Creator of the world and your Creator . . ." I answered thee as was fitting, and is fitting for the whole of Israel who knew these things, first from personal experience, and afterwards through uninterrupted tradition, which is equal to the former.'

(He claims the superiority of his faith by pointing to the witness of the prophets.) 'If we find a man who walks into the fire without hurt, abstains from food for some time without starving, on whose face a light shines which the eye cannot bear, who is never ill, nor ages, until his life's natural end . . . is such a degree not visibly distinguished from the ordinary human degree? . . . These are some of the characteristics of the undoubted prophets through whom God made Himself manifest . . .'[2]

'Our belief is comprised in the Torah – a very large domain.' What lies at the root of the essential discipline that constitutes man's duty to God in the Jewish faith is – obedience. This provides a clue to the character and purpose of the Torah, the codified way of life that is laid upon Israel as a binding obligation. It is an instrument for the shaping of a people which is to express God's purpose in the world. The moral or ethical part of the Code, at first laid down as an external command, became as its lessons were learned something that pious men could recognize as part of their own nature, something that must and could be realized in the life of a whole people. The ceremonial or ritual part of its content on the other hand does not have to pass the bar of man's reason: since its ultimate meaning lies in the demand for obedience, the response is to be measured by the purity of its motive rather than by the character of the actions that express it. Not conformity as such, but dedication is the key. Here is what led Pascal to say, 'The entire religion of Israel consisted only of the love of God'.

Given the fundamental character of Judaism as an infinite demand laid upon a particular body of people, it becomes easier to understand the specific tensions which have always marked its history, and are now revealed in their contemporary forms in the Jewish State. We will note four. One is the tension between eternal truth and secular change, or between spiritual law and formulated code, which underlies the bitter contemporary conflict about fixity of ritual observance. Then there is collective and individual obligation, expressed in today's soul-searchings about the relation between the values of socialism, or Labour-Zionism, and those of religion. Next comes the tension between the exclusive and the universal aspects of the mission of Israel, revealed in sharp differences about the right of the people to its Land and the way this should be safeguarded. Lastly, and underlying the interminable argument about Jewish identity, is the question whether Judaism is nationality or religion; or if it is both, how so, and with what practical implications.

REVELATION AND CHANGE

The earlier part of the story of how the Torah shaped a people is told in the narratives and prophetic utterances of the Bible itself. Between the return from the purifying experience of the Babylonian exile and the Roman conquest Judaism was developed by the Jewish people.

They were led by priests and scribes, and were moved by a determination to preserve untainted the vision of the patriarchs, Moses and the prophets. During these centuries the people's mode of thought was changed through the life of the synagogue and the schools. It is a tale of radical progress. In the days of the prophets, as the Bible record makes clear, crude idolatry was a constant and aggressive menace, calling for incessant denunciation and warning. Towards the end of the Second Temple, as the New Testament records show and the Scrolls confirm, Jews were accusing one another of many grievous sins, but paganism was not among them. Idolatry as an interior threat had been cast out and the Jews had shown themselves equipped and eager to resist successive attempts to foist it on them.

This moral growth and development during the period of the Second Temple was reflected in the reformulation and amplification of the code of law itself. New conditions called for its adaptation and adjustment. There grew up an increasing body of interpretative provisions, which sought to relate scriptural injunctions to constantly changing circumstances. Most scholars now accept the view that this oral law was originally a bridge between Scripture and current fact, that it was inspired by a constant attempt to discover a scriptural warrant for provisions newly required, and that it showed the vitality of the Jewish faith, inspired by its traditional teaching but not enslaved to it.

Louis Finkelstein, the leading Jewish writer of today on the Pharisees, said of one of the greatest of them, Akiba, 'It is obvious that he considered the interpretation of the written law merely the form which had to be followed in the derivation of desirable rules from the scriptural text.' This is a startlingly modern, and 'modernist', version of the meaning of scriptural authority.

How does God speak to man day by day? Does He point him, for practical guidance, backward to the texts or forward to tomorrow's inspiration? To any believer in the authority of written documents it is no easy question. G. F. Moore, one of the most sympathetic and discerning of Christian commentators on Judaism, wrote:

The application of modern historical and critical methods to the Scriptures, *and above all the introduction of the idea of development* involves, consciously or unconsciously, a complete change in the idea of revelation, a change which orthodoxy, whether Jewish or Christian, has resisted with the instinct of self-preservation.[3]

To a Jew of tradition the issue certainly was a disputable one. It was in fact fought over during the century or two before Gospel times, with the Sadducees as partisans of the strictly backward look, accepting only scriptural authority in all its rigidity, and the Pharisees as believers in and practitioners of adaptation and adjustment. The Pharisees won: the Sadducees and their doctrine vanished. The tradition itself was reformulated over the two centuries and a half after the fall of Jerusalem in AD 70. The innovating, creative spirit of the Tannaite rabbis who did the work had as free scope as was consistent with some sort of adherence to the authority of the Pentateuch. Even that proviso did not always apply. The rabbis said: 'When the times demand that something be done for the Lord, a provision of the Torah may be made void.'[4]

What then became of all this openness of mind? Why was the code of the later Tannaite rabbis supposed to end innovative thinking? (Of course it did not end the process of elaboration and study.) The answer may be the same as that to the question why the biblical canon itself was terminated with the 'prophetic' book of Daniel. It would seem that the reason was not a matter of doctrine but of history, and the historical motive was the defence of the essence of the faith itself against fierce external pressures. In the case of the scriptural canon, the invading force was Hellenism. In the case of the Talmud, it was Christianity, and the backlash of Roman dictatorship. A fair conclusion might be that Judaism, though bound in a sense to documents and to a tradition, is not inherently rigid in its attitudes, and becomes so only at times when the essence of the teaching or – more urgently – the survival of the community charged with its preservation, is held to be endangered by controversy and change.

PEOPLE AND PERSON

In what sense are the written law (Torah) and its elaboration in the so-called oral law (Halacha) collective rather than individual: for a people rather than for persons? In the ancient world all religion was originally the religion of a community, as the supposed etymology of the Latin word itself suggests – *religio*, a binding tie. Any man who takes religion seriously must assume that the same thing will be true in some sense, when the day comes that spiritual values are acknowledged as supreme in every province of life. Modern civilization is founded in practice on the opposite assumption – that the religious and the civil are separate provinces, and that a man's pursuits and his persuasion do not much overlap. Judaism denies this; inevitably so because an elected people, called upon to obey a rule of observance, requires that the rule itself be collective in its application. On the other hand, in the Hebrew Bible after the five books of Moses the trend of the teaching is away from collective and towards individual responsibility – at least in the sphere of the moral code – and the shift from one to the other is explicitly declared by the prophets.

Yet many of the moral maxims of the Levitical code concern matters in which individual obedience would be impossible except in the context of acceptance and observance by the community. These maxims were held generally binding (with some need for adjustment) as long as the Jewish people lived as a community in its own land. When it no longer made its own civil laws the sages continued to discuss both the principles and the details of the corporate code, against the day when these would again be practical politics. Much of the provision for ceremonial and ritual observance was also collective in its implication: and by its nature this at least could be observed under foreign civil domination, and in the ghetto. It remained the witness to Israel's will to adhere to the covenant, and the fact that in due course it became the only part of that witness that could still be borne, gave to its observance a still more intense dedication.

The simple fact is that in traditional Judaism individual and collective obedience are two sides of a single coin: their separation, like the separation of moral from ritual obedience, could only distort the character of each and cut their common taproot. This is why today those Zionists who are religious can be content with no way of life that denies to their faith the opportunity of full corporate expression, and why non-religious ones constantly try to embody in social institutions and conduct the ingrained moral values of the ancestral tradition.

EXCLUSIVE OR UNIVERSAL?

From the very outset the ultimate inconsistency between the worship of one supreme God and a doctrine of exclusiveness was recognized and expressed in the narratives. Abram the founding patriarch was sent out to father a nation, but the climax of the promises made to him was 'in thee shall all the families of the earth be blessed'. The revelation on

Sinai was, according to the teaching itself, not exclusive to those present. In Moses' words, declaring the will of the Lord: 'It is not with you alone that I am making this covenant and this oath, but with all those who stand here with us today before the Lord our God, and also with those who are not here with us today.'[5] There can, on the other hand, be no questioning the many scriptural declarations of Israel's separateness, of the gulf between it and other nations, indeed of its superiority. All of this has always had, and still has, its weight in the tradition and the way it is regarded. It figures constantly in present day liturgy. But equally beyond doubt are the repeated and increasingly incisive prophetic declarations that the message, and indeed the promise, are for all mankind. These culminated in Isaiah's many references to universal salvation. None of these denied the significance of Election and Covenant. The implication was rather that the nations would respond to the inspiration and leadership of Israel as a priestly people. But one remarkable declaration of Isaiah goes even beyond that: 'Some of them [gentiles] I will take for priests, for Levites, says the Lord.'[6] It is true that universal religion was always envisioned as universal Judaism: this was inevitable, and was actually the opposite of exclusive. Judaism and religion must have been to the Hebrews one and the same. No modern heir of their spiritual tradition, whatever his present day adherence, could quarrel with that assumption in the pagan world of its day.

So, as with other cruxes, in the developed forms of Judaism particularism (or exclusivity) and universalism were and are two sides of one fact: election finding its purpose in world-wide mission, universalism finding its way to realization through the priestly witness of one group. The exclusiveness can be more apparent than real: in the loftiest vision it is transcended in the universal end it serves. Yet it is bound to remain for human beings in a human society dangerous doctrine, calling for the noblest and most selfless level of thought to save it from arrogance.

The claim to divine Election and Mission is not palatable to reflective non-Jewish opinion, indeed not credible to it. But when Election is seen as a heavy burden – as it certainly has been in most of the teaching, if not perhaps always in all the practice – and above all when it is seen as forfeit unless continually earned, it becomes to others a tolerable idea, at least as a standard by which the performance of the claimants can be judged. That however is the outside view. If one makes the effort of imagination needed to see the doctrine as the faithful Jew sees it, one begins to be aware of the constant tension he must feel between the call to be a light to the gentiles, and the need to fence off and jealously guard not only the teaching itself but the life of the people as its witnesses. Here we come to the great, inherent, unresolved dilemma.

NATIONALITY AND RELIGION

In the history of Israel, as Jews are taught it and shaped by it, the dilemma appeared very early. As soon as the natural unity of a tribal group or federation began to reveal its inadequacy in more complex conditions, division of mind showed itself. The institution of kingship was founded upon a split thought. There are two official versions of the change from the rule of Judges to that of Kings. Common to the two is the wish of the people to copy from surrounding tribes the institution of monarchy, which would defend them more effectively against their enemies. In the first version Samuel, symbol of the rule of God's law, warned them under the Lord's direction of the cost of kingship in money and lost liberty, but yielded finally to their insistence. But, in the second, the Lord Himself endorses Saul's appointment. 'He shall deliver my people from the Philistines. I have seen the sufferings of my people and their cry has reached my ears.'[7] The whole of the later history of the Hebrews in their own land could be read as an elaboration of that foundational clash between the acceptance of the Law as Ruler and the yearning for a political instrument of survival. The conflict is alive in Israel today.

In the history of the people, as they saw it and lived by it, David came nearest to reconciling the dual allegiance. But he was not allowed to forget its duality: his dear ambition to build a temple for the God he served was denied him because of the military achievement that had made the project feasible: 'You have shed much blood in my sight and waged great wars; for this reason you shall not build a house in honour of my name.'[8] It seems hard. Indeed the spiritual demand does bear hardly on men of the world; but it belongs to the Tradition as much as do the Maccabees and Massada. This too figures in lively public discussion in today's state.

Through later centuries the secular tendencies of a kingly state and the spiritual call of prophecy clashed again and again, until the final catastrophe of the exile to Babylon. The spiritual rebirth that followed did not however impair the sense of nationhood, at least among the minority of exiles who fostered and carried out 'a vigorous proto-Zionist movement', establishing their state once again behind its defensive walls, on that 'hillock in Zion' which was also mysteriously the dwelling place of the Infinite. More than physical safety had to be ensured: one of the restored community's first measures was to cast out the gentile wives whose influence threatened the integrity of Judaism from within, as Sanballat and his allies had threatened it from without. The defence in each case was the Law, first enjoined upon the military defenders, then enforced against the erring citizens.

During the five or six centuries that span the period from the end of the biblical record to the Emperor Hadrian's final destruction of Jerusalem in AD 135, Jewish history, though 'essentially that of their religion', showed them twice driven in its defence into the assertion of quasi-independent nationhood. Then nationalist values would threaten to corrupt the purity of the faith, whose guardians would withdraw support from the secular power or turn against it. The plainest instance was the successful Maccabean revolt against Antiochus Epiphanes' attempt to impose pagan practices on the Temple cult. The monarchs whose throne was established by the victory, though at first hailed as the symbols and guarantors of hard-won religious freedom and national independence, went the way of so many of their predecessors before the Captivity. They turned to secular ambitions and paths. The Hasidaeans, the pietists who had helped Judas Maccabeus to victory, in disgust turned back to their synagogues and to the keeping of the Law. Their successors, the early Pharisees, the increasingly well organized 'religious party' of the day, rejected the aggressive, expansionist ideas of two successive monarchs – or rather rejected the secular impact of such ideas within the religious life of the State. In the end their disillusion with what these descendants of the Maccabees had made of the once-prized monarchy contributed directly to its downfall and to Pompey's conquest of the land in 63 BC.

Under Roman rule in the next hundred years, until the second conquest by Titus, the same tendencies revealed themselves. The Pharisees, to whom their faith and its observance were the paramount concern, were content to live quietly under an alien rule which conceded them their religious rights. To the Romans these were a national cult which they were bound under their own imperial code to respect as such, even though it was to them absurd, even potentially dangerous.

But the militants were not content with religious concessions. To them the separation of religion and nation was a constant threat to the former and an intolerable wrong; their tempers simmered on the edge of revolt and occasionally boiled over. They opposed the political appeasement of the Romans practised by the subservient King Herod, and even found it hard that he should bargain with his overlords for religious concessions. In the background of the thoughts of many of them were apocalyptic visions of an ideal national future, the path to which called for the overthrow of the Romans by military means. In human terms this was of course utterly unrealistic, but God could be counted on for a miracle. These dreams bred a recklessness which led directly to the war of AD 66-70. It ended in utter defeat, the selling of Jerusalem's population into slavery, the destruction of the Temple, the mass suicide at Massada. But it also saw the initiation at Jamnia or Yavne of the rabbinical school which codified the oral law, and gave to Judaism the form its orthodoxy still wears.

For a few decades after AD 70 Palestine was comparatively peaceful. But when Hadrian began to pursue a more active policy of cultural Hellenization, and there was even talk of prohibiting circumcision, revolt broke out again. The rebel leader Bar Kochba fought for three years but was finally crushed. Jerusalem was destroyed and replaced by a pagan city. Its people were banished to the remoter parts of the land. The most eminent rabbi of the day, Akiba, supported the revolt and died a martyr's death. The Jewish Christians of Palestine, however, who had been living for a century as a more or less tolerated, more or less heretical sect within the Jewish fold, had refused to play any part in the revolt. This was the ultimate offence: from then on they were utterly and finally cast out. It is one of the most momentous consequences of this final outburst of Judaism in its national aspect, that it completed the rift between the two religions and made it irreversible, at least for that age and long after.

The end of the Jewish State of classical times brings a natural break in this record of a thousand years of tension and conflict between the two aspects of Judaism. Perhaps the real crux, certainly the most dramatic expression of it, came in AD 70. At Massada nationalist hopes were outwardly crushed but the flame of militant heroism burnt ineffaceably bright. At Jamnia, in the same year, under the conqueror's permissive hand, was founded the great rabbinical school which rescued the oral law from oblivion and began the process of refinement and codification that still keeps it alive in the Talmud. What was the mysterious blend of these two that made of Judaism the only force in the ancient world which could withstand the all-pervading spirit of Hellenism with its character unimpaired, and long outlast the Hellenic nations? Why did Judaism, though it suffered Roman subjugation as did the Greeks, not transform the thought of its conquerors as they did, yet achieve, as they did not, an organic survival? By what vital secret does it exist today, still embodied in the only people of the vast Roman world that has preserved unchanged its faith, its communal life, even its name? *language!*

The questions are unanswered. They remain as the key to the troubled inner life of the ancient people in its modern state.

2

AD 135—1945

'The work of the Pharisees bore fruit. They succeeded in creating a sort of shadowy body politic, with no roots in solid earth; and within this shadowy framework the Hebrew national spirit has lived its own distinctive life for two thousand years.' These words can serve as the link between the end of the last Jewish nation state and the first practical stirrings that led to its restoration: fittingly, they came in 1904 from the pen of Ahad Ha'am, one of the early and perhaps the most effective of the heralds of rebirth. The writer was in fact – and the point is worth noting – contrasting the annihilation of the purely political hopes of Jewry with the unimpaired survival of its communal life as a people of faith and observance.

During the greater part of 1800 years Jews nurtured their religion in a secular darkness ranging from bare toleration and exploited semi-serfdom to savage persecution. This was not the whole story: they lived peaceful and constructive lives not only in Babylon, Egypt and Northern Africa, but in the Muslim communities of Spain for five centuries, from the ninth to the fourteenth, and among Christians in Mediterranean Europe in the early Middle Ages. For the rest it was otherwise. Their interior history, however, was not frozen. There was the confrontation with Aristotelean philosophy (mediated at first through the thought of Islam in its prime) and the long accompanying argument about the relation of faith to reason. There was the rise of mysticism in its various phases from the early Kabbalists to the Hasidim of Eastern Europe in the eighteenth century and onwards – a loud and significant counterpoint to the conformist life of the normal communities. There were modifications and adaptations by great medieval and later sages in the classical readings of the halacha. But always there were two cords of continuity. One was the undefeated yearning for a return to the Land of Promise; for some, this was to be realized by prayer in the Almighty's good time: for others (the usual division) to

17

be effected by personal pilgrimage or communal 'Aliya'. The second link was an essential uniformity of life, east and west, north and south, based on the habit of passionate study of the Law and on a commonly recognized legal system. Thrown on their own resources, denied full membership in Christian and Muslim societies, they developed methods of local and regional self-government and legal autonomy derived from the divinely sanctioned precepts of the Mosaic Law and the Talmud, and practised throughout the whole world of Jewry. Not all regional codes were identical but all were accepted universally as legitimately Jewish. By the time the eighteenth century was reached there was a remarkable resemblance in the patterns of life of the various widely separated communities in their disparate national surroundings: a widespread common culture based on traditional studies, on patterns of daily life if not uniform then bearing strong family likenesses, and a social pattern in which the Rabbi everywhere stood at or near the summit.

It shows how isolated Jewish life was from its surroundings that a people not without intellectual gifts or receptivity should have remained for two centuries so little touched, especially outside Italy, by the violent ferment of ideas that followed on the New Learning and the Renaissance. But at length the secular beams did break through, first in eighteenth-century Germany, then – after the explosive impact of the French Revolution – throughout Western Europe. In one country after another the ghetto walls crumbled, undermined by the new social and intellectual forces. There were phases of reaction, but as the nineteenth century unfolded legal equality was gradually achieved and Jews increasingly took their places in the lives of their countries. The process of assimilation began, in all degrees from decreasing observance to total conversion. It is thought that during the nineteenth century a quarter of a million German Jews adopted Christianity. Compromise forms of Jewish organization and synagogal practice developed. One movement, under the leadership of a Frankfurt rabbi S. R. Hirsch, claimed to have found a way to combine fairly full participation in secular society with strict adherence to traditional faith and practice. This sort of approach found favour in several countries, and the amalgam flourished while the ancient way of the ghetto inevitably faded out. The call of Jerusalem itself was drowned by the dissonant clamour of an age of material learning, material progress and the materialist conception of history.

To all this there was one massive exception, which was of crucial significance for the future situation of Judaism and Jewry in the world. We have sketched the change in Western Europe. But more than half the Jews in the whole world lived to the East. By the end of the nineteenth century there were well over half a million Jews in Germany and nearly a quarter of a million in England. But in Russia and Poland, which had by then already lost a million and a half Jews to the New World, there still remained more than five millions, penned in a vast social ghetto that ran from the Oder to the Dnieper. Under compulsion, they lived a life of their own, ground between the millstones of a repressive landowning aristocracy and an illiterate peasantry open to every gust of racialist passion or propaganda. In England, a Jew was increasingly becoming an Englishman of the Jewish faith: in Germany, the same. But the Jew in Russia (except for a scattering of the wealthy in the big cities) was not even tempted to think of himself as a Russian, except in the sense that it was Russian citizenship of whose rights he was deprived. He belonged to a community which, outside the provinces of government and civil law, had all the marks of nationhood: it had its own popular art, something of its own literature, unmistakably its own language. It was the only community in the world in which a Jew could not merely drift away from his religion or be indifferent to it, but actively reject and combatively oppose it, and still see himself and be seen by others as recognizably and meaningfully a Jew. It was here that secular Judaism was born.

There were a great many who did reject and oppose. If they were intellectuals, they were moved partly by the new positivist, humanist ideas growing out of Western science and Darwinism. Living in a community in which religion meant strict adherence to the Talmud, with no bridge between this and Western culture, no third choice beyond medieval tradition or atheism, under a regime of persecution or at best gross injustice, they were wide open to any creed, however dogmatic or disruptive, that offered the prospect of release. There were in fact two such creeds.

One was the heady doctrine of nationalism, which arose like a phoenix from the ashes of revolutionary France and spread its wings over much of Europe. One Jewish scholar, Jacob Talmon, has suggested that there was a particular affinity between nationalism and the Jewish spirit, which had originally provided for the new 'religion' the seminal idea of the divine right of a people to its freedom – 'the people of God fighting God's battles'. The same authority has also pointed out the sensitive response of Jewish nationalist sentiment in Russia to the successive triumphs of embattled nationalism in Greece, Serbia, Italy, Bulgaria: every one of the historic statements of Zionist philosophy came in the aftermath of the victory of some national movement. It needs little imagination to see how this liberating idea must have worked upon the hearts and minds of many a thoughtful, sensitive young Jew, his ancestral group feeling alive within him but starved of its normal nourishment in a vigorous, well-rounded communal life.

The other crusading idea was socialism, in two versions. One was the creed of class struggle, needing no reinforcement from Jewish sentiment as such – indeed opposed to it: the second was a special form of it, complicated by resentment against the anti-Semitism of a ruling class which not only cherished the sentiment but used it deliberately to incite the peasant mobs, whom their rapacity kept half-starved, against a defenceless body of aliens. It was this very defencelessness that provided the climate of feeling in which not only the sense of social and economic grievance but the idea of nationalism itself could flourish and blossom into the will to act. Not that the sense of grievance necessarily took practical form as Zionism: indeed there were Jewish socialists who attacked Zionism as what would now be called a bourgeois deviation: a piece of escapism: a desertion of the workers in a battle that must be fought and won in the land where oppression held sway. But for Jewish nationalism, whether or not it was entwined with the sense of social wrong, there could be only one positive course. It led towards Palestine. Down that road those who felt their people's immemorial longing for the Holy Land, those who heard its call as the voice of Israel's God, those who thought first of Jewry's need for a place in the sun (and did not doubt where the sun shone brightest for the Jew), and those individual Jews who sought the most hopeful escape from intolerable oppression, could all walk together.

Plainly, much of the ferment in Russia was boiling and bubbling before Herzl published his manifesto *Judenstaat* in 1896. But it was then, when he began to apply his gifts as propagandist and politician to the task of giving practical form to the idea of a return to Palestine, that Zionism made an effective appearance on the world stage, and some of those with hands on the levers of power began to take note. Herzl himself was a man of ideas, but he was not an ideologue of Judaism. He has been described as 'born secularised'. He was concerned, not with the manifest destiny of the Jewish people as such, but with the plight of Jews. When the iniquities of the Dreyfus trial roused in him the conviction that a total escape from gentile society was the one hope for Jews, he knew nothing of the nationalist theorizing in Eastern Europe. He betrayed no knowledge that Leo Pinsker had, sixteen years before *Judenstaat* appeared, published a book called *Auto-Emancipation* in which, with considerable imaginative and analytical power, he connected anti-Semitism with Jewry's lack of a landbase and a state. This may have left Pinsker, as later thinkers argued, the 'real' founder of political Zionism: but those very quotation marks, and the fact that nothing much happened for sixteen years, show the greatness of Herzl's practical achievement, and the need for workaday methods to bring prophetic visions to earth. If one had to find a formula to cover the historic beginnings of Zionism, it might be that Pinsker had the idea, Herzl created the institutions and found the wherewithal, and Ahad Ha'am's message inspired his fellow Russians to go and start the hard work.

That work had begun, less arduously, with a few late-nineteenth-century settlements, financed by millionaire philanthropists in England and France, drawing their manpower both from Europe and from the local religious communities in the 'holy cities' of Jerusalem, Safed, Tiberias and Hebron. By 1900 Palestine's Jewish population was about 60,000, mostly in these four cities and Jaffa, with some small groups elsewhere and the handful of settlements on the land. These were workers but employed Arab labour, which marked off both their economy and their ideology sharply from the real beginnings of Zionist settlement. That came with the Second Aliyah – the trickle of Russians who came either to solve the 'Jewish problem' in their own land, or to restore their own personality by working that land, or to give practical expression to their Marxist ideology – or any combination of these motives. In her inaugural speech as Prime Minister, Mrs Meir in 1969 paid her tribute to 'that wonderful band of the Second Aliyah. They were not the first to revolt against Diaspora life, but they dared to turn rebellion into a great action, the implementation by their own effort of a revolution in the nation's life.'

Among them were a President-to-be and two Prime Ministers of the future Jewish state. Ben-Gurion has given his own definition of their aim: 'To attach themselves to the soil of their homeland and to live a life of honest work in an atmosphere of comradeship and freedom and within a framework of equality.'[1] This was the germ of the Kibbutz, and of much that has been characteristic of life in Israel. The men who founded Deganya, the 'mother of the kibbutzim' (at the southern end of Lake Galilee, in a district where the early Jewish Christians are

believed to have practised communal living) were for the most part in
revolt against what they termed religion – the conservative clericalism
they had known in the ghetto. But the aim that Ben-Gurion described
owed at least as much to the Jewish ideal of justice as to the Marxist
creed. 'Long before I took office as Prime Minister my goal was the
creation of a model society, which could become, in the language of the
Biblical prophets, a light unto the nations.'[2]

Most of the Zionist pioneers would have shied away from anything
that suggested religious inspiration. Their idea was to get away from
sectarianism and help to build a nation. But Buber was to write of the
Palestinian pioneer that whether he knows and likes it or not 'he is
animated by the age-old Jewish longing to incorporate social truth in
the lives of individuals living with one another'.[3]

This was a special kind of secularism and of socialism. If one is to
penetrate its inner significance more deeply, and to see these bare
historical data in their relation to what was actually to happen in
Palestine and Israel, it is necessary to disentangle and examine further
the underlying ideas that were at work. One must first distinguish two
different approaches to Jewish history and (by the same token) to the
meaning of Jewish identity. One of these is based on the idea of divine
election, the other on the historical (or in the current jargon the
existential) fact of a people's life and activity. The distinction may or
may not be ultimately valid: we have found some reason to think that
Judaism rests on the premise that it is not. But it has at least some
provisional viability and some expository value.

Let it not be supposed that Election is a doctrine held only by religious
Jews, who believe in the Covenant at Sinai as a historic fact. The
history of Zionism, and much current public discussion in the State of
Israel, prove otherwise. There are of course traditionally religious
Zionists: one could in a sense apply that term to all the faithful whose
thoughts through the centuries have turned constantly towards Zion
as the focus of a people's memory and the lodestar of its dreams. There
were also those European rabbis and others who quite early in the
nineteenth century adumbrated practical ideas about return. And there
have been, and are, later believers who have backed their faith with
their working lives, on Kibbutzim or in the cities, making it a deliberate
personal choice to fulfil the Lord's will for his people, and through
them for the world, in the Land He promised. This is one of the
orthodox views of Election and Return. But the messianic view of the
role of Israel can also take a form that does not call itself religious at all.

There was, as an early exemplar, Moses Hess (1812–75) who perceived as Jewish destiny a special civilizing mission, or at least a special part in the general civilizing task laid upon Western man. This task in Israel's case was to guard that nodal area in the Middle East with which so much of the fate of nations seems to be involved, and to educate and raise up the backward peoples of the region. Hess would not have been happy to rest his case on the fact that Isaiah saw it first; but the continuity of the dream or vision is interesting. 'When that day comes Israel shall rank with Egypt and Assyria, those three, and shall be a blessing in the centre of the world. So the Lord of Hosts will bless them: A blessing be upon Egypt my people, upon Assyria the work of my hands, and upon Israel my possession.'[4]

Pinsker has been mentioned. Then there was Borochov, the quasi-Marxist [1881–1907], who thought it necessary to build the State of Israel so as to enable the Jewish people to play its own unique part in the international class struggle.

Above all, there was Ahad Ha'am, 'One of the people', the pen-name of Asher Ginzberg who from 1889, when he was thirty-three, to his death in Tel-Aviv in 1927, fulfilled more nearly than any other man the role of prophet of secular Zionism, the nationalist creed of destiny which we are describing. It is best to let him speak of it in his own way. 'I should say that religion itself is only one of the forms of culture and that Judaism is neither the one nor the other, but is the national creative power, which in the past expressed itself in a primarily religious culture.' 'It is obvious that a national culture cannot come into existence, and cannot create a new type of life, if it is purely spiritual. It must obviously include all the elements necessary to a nation, from agricultural labourers and craftsmen to the purest intellectuals.' 'The whole point of the material settlement – whether its architects realise it or not – is to provide the foundation for that spiritual centre of our nation which is destined to arise in Palestine in response to the insistent urge of the national instinct.' 'Our national creative power . . . remains the same in all ages, and it has not ceased even in exile to work in its own specific fashion.' There are two key ideas: the national creative power inherent in the Jewish people, which he terms spiritual but does not connect with religion, and the need to give this an embodiment in the Land.

Ahad Ha'am argued long and persistently against the idea that the National Home was primarily a place of refuge for the oppressed. It came about that as such a refuge, for the victims of Nazism, it took its great leap forward in numbers, and in the impulsion towards full independence. But that by no means proves the prophet wrong. Had it not been for the vision of a land, and a community, in which the Jewish spirit could strike root and flourish, there might not have been a Palestine to which those in flight from the Nazi camps could turn for protection and nourishment. Yet a question about the reality behind Ahad Ha'am's vision remains to vex us. What is this national creative power? When he looks for a tangible witness Ahad Ha'am refers to the Bible and the Talmud, monuments to the religious spirit. When he speaks of a national creative power which remains the same through all ages, he seems either to be uttering a disguised religious credo or making an idol of that racialist myth, born of the infant crudities of nineteenth-century biology, of which the twentieth century has had more than enough. The point is profoundly important for the life of Israel, and we shall return to it. For the moment it is enough to remark that the prophetic message of secular Zionism may not have been as secular as the prophet supposed.

Another figure in the Zionist pantheon, another who took an idealized view of the return to the Holy Land, yet would not call himself religious, is Aaron David Gordon. It is at first puzzling that a man who would set up as his standard the ideal of a people made in the image of God, preach the loftiest ethical doctrines, and proclaim the gospel of work on the land as a means of renewing the severed link not only between the Jewish people and its ancestral home but between modern man and the cosmos, should not be reckoned religious. Gordon's co-workers, vigorous young 'atheists' straight from some Marxist schoolroom, did in fact sometimes jeer at his convictions. But it was he himself who dismissed the idea that the case against assimilation, which was part of the case for the return to Zion, rested on religious grounds. The reason he saw was national sentiment – 'a primal force within every one of us, which is fighting for its own life, which seeks its own realisation . . . our ethnic self, the cosmic element . . . which . . . forms one of the basic ingredients of the personality of each and every one of us.' Here again is the Jewish identity, the 'Jewish soul' set up as an absolute, over against the religious tradition which, in its own view, had shaped and preserved it. At this point we do no more than take note of the phenomenon, which completes this brief reference to the unique doctrine of secular Zionism, with its non-metaphysical claim to metaphysical 'otherness', its messianism with no messiah, its Election without an Elector.

The most extreme case of "secular Zionism"

There is also a separate version of secular Zionism which, at least ostensibly, discards the whole concept of Election. These are the secularists *pur sang*, who conceive the Jewish people neither as the Chosen of God nor as the creators of their history by their innate genius, but as the product of that history. The Jews are a people hammered into recognizable shape by millennia of suffering. They are a 'community of fate', a 'family' whose inner bond is formed not by the flesh but by a religious cult which it has, with unusual tenacity, employed as its instrument of corporate survival. Given this, the Jewish people need no more of theory to explain them than do thousands of millions of other human families deposited as waifs of time on the doorstep of the future. What will become of them, whether and how their character and outlook may change, are questions not to be answered *a priori*: they lie covered, in the lap of destiny.

A writer named Jacob Klatzkin, about the time of the first world war, clarified this picture in his own way. 'This is its originality – that Judaism depends on form and not content . . . Either the Jewish people shall redeem the land and thereby continue to live, even if the spiritual content of Judaism changes radically, or we shall remain in exile and rot away, even if the spiritual tradition continues to exist.' Indeed the 'spiritual' content is found to be a danger to Jews and others – both crippling and chauvinistic. The basic contention of Zionism is 'to deny any concept of Jewish identity based on spiritual criteria'. 'Zionism pins its hopes on the general advance of civilisation, and its national faith is also a faith in man in general, faith in the power of the good and the beautiful.' But even this determined rider seems to baulk at the last fence: although 'we are neither a denomination nor a school of thought, but members of one family, bearers of a common history', yet 'the national definition too requires an act of will'. Besides 'the compulsion of history' there is 'a will expressed in that history'. Are we back again in the realm of spiritualized biology?

So much for speculation on the meaning of secular Jewishness. Let us turn away from it now to examine our first category of all, those Jews who accept the doctrine of Election on purely religious grounds and reject Zionism. The place to start is, once again, the Emancipation of the nineteenth century, the sharp secular sword-stroke that cut across and half-severed the continuing thread of the history of Judaism. Could the vision of a grand cosmic drama performed under divine authority, with the Jews in the central role, survive the onslaught of modern scholarship, and the new conception of evolutionary development? There was an approach – that of S. R. Hirsch – which could cling to orthodoxy and accept Emancipation as simply the latest phase of challenge in the historic mission of Israel, a phase of adaptation to the superficialities of secular thought and life, a new obstacle to be surmounted. But Hirsch himself exempted the documentary sources of Judaism from the attentions of critical scholarship: sacrosanct, they were to be studied only in order to reveal their meaning further. Strict obedience to the Torah remained the paramount obligation and there could be no re-possession of the Promised Land, no achievement of national status, till all was fulfilled in a new messianic era. Thus for his followers traditional Judaism was safeguarded, along with the right of faithful Jews in Germany to stay comfortably put.

But even this was at least an acknowledgment of the right of the new secular culture to exist. Much further east than Frankfurt, and not so long after Hirsch himself flourished, the new ideas were as we have seen emerging in more and more menacing form. Modern Zionism was born. The orthodox in the ghettos saw its threat to the old order in sharp focus, and their opposition to it was total. As one of many[5] we can allow the Dzikover Rebbe, speaking in 1900 from his orthodox fastness, to strike the note and set the scene:

> For our many sins, strangers have risen to pasture the holy flock,
> men who say that the people of Israel should be clothed in secular
> nationalism, a nation like all other nations, that Judaism rests on
> three things, national feeling, the land and the language, and that
> national feeling is the most praiseworthy element in the brew and
> the most effective in preserving Judaism, while the observance of
> the Torah and the commandments is a private matter depending
> on the inclination of each individual. May the Lord rebuke these
> evil men and may he who chooseth Jerusalem seal their mouths.[6]

The Rebbe plainly understood what confronted him, and knew how to make his point.

It was in Germany, under the influence of Hirsch's ideas, that the backlash of orthodoxy first took organized shape, in the formation of Agudat Israel; the idea soon spread eastward, and was given the powerful authority of the rabbinical leaders of the Hasidist and Moralist movements, such as the Rebbe just quoted. In their apocalyptic fashion these men saw the new development as a phase in Satan's increasing war against God's design for His people. The earlier plan to undermine their strength by assimilation was being foiled by anti-Semitism: so

Satan was producing a new device, to turn even the solid strength of Jewish feeling into a weakness by separating it from religious teaching and opposing the two. More cunningly still, he was inspiring some orthodox leaders to proclaim that the fulfilment of the Zionist ideal would act as a focus for religious loyalty and help to bring lapsed Jews back to the fold.

It was these men, the 'religious Zionists', seen by Agudat Israel as Satan's dupes, who in 1911 founded Mizrachi, 'the first organised religious-political party in Jewish history', the beginning of a movement that is now the chief religious prop of the government of the State of Israel.

At that time, as at many later stages in Israel, and to some extent still today, Mizrachi was too 'secular' for some of the devout, who withdrew to join Aguda. Under eminent religious patronage, this movement held its first general conference in 1912 and then, after the complete disruption of international relations during the first world war, called another 'Grand Assembly' in Vienna in 1923. By this time the Balfour Declaration had ushered in a new era and the British were in the saddle: these *faits accomplis* caused some internal differences in Aguda, between spiritual hardliners and those who thought Zionist organization and methods should be matched by its foes. But the whole movement, slight though its impact was in Western Europe, became in the East an organized propagandist instrument, a powerful counterforce to the Zionist trend.

In Palestine itself, developments of a very different kind were under way. In accordance with Muslim polity, Turkish rule had allowed every religious community to conduct its own affairs in matters of special concern to religion, notably questions of family status (marriage, divorce, etc.). When the Turks were driven out in 1917 and the British Mandatory Government was set up, it followed the *laissez faire* tradition of British colonial policy which took over the institutional systems it found, especially if they were as congenial as this one. For civil administration it found nothing, and later organized a representative system with some fiscal powers. But for religious purposes it dealt from the outset with the organized Jewish community under its Rabbinate, as with the Muslims and Christians, treating as a community member whoever wished to be so and was accepted. Such a system demanded centralization of authority within the religious community, and the Mizrachi party, the religious Zionists, were in a strong position. Two Chief Rabbis were appointed, one Sephardi, one Ashkenazi:

the first holder of the latter post was the famous Rabbi Kook, a scholar and mystic and a strong believer in the national idea. An administrative pattern was laid down, including a central court of appeal from the judgments of rabbinical courts. This whole system, and the very considerable power and influence it conferred on the party in possession, was too much for most of the independent religious communities. However, one intransigent group went on defying official policy, in the name of the authority of the Torah, and though it was refused official recognition its members were allowed to opt out of the recognized Jewish community and accept the normal services from their own organization. It called itself, finally, the Orthodox Community (Edah Haredit), and it was adopted as the Palestine branch of Aguda's European headquarters. By this time Hitlerite persecution was well on its murderous course: the pressure on German and Austrian Jews to get out if they could was irresistible, the stream of demand for certificates of entry became a flood, and the Jewish Agency not unnaturally favoured those who were prepared to collaborate with the Zionists in Israel. This undermined the positions of the ultra-orthodox dissidents both in Europe and Palestine, and the local leadership had to make for its membership the best terms it could with ruling officialdom. The pill to be swallowed was less bitter in that the leaders themselves, without departing from their vision of the cosmic drama of Israel, could, as the Nazi horror developed, envisage the return of the persecuted as a unique conjunction of divine purpose and human need. They could even – after the cataclysm of the world war, and the Nazi death camps – acknowledge the foundation of the State itself as 'the beginning of the Redemption', and as chief spokesman for the interests of full religious orthodoxy could play a part in the settlement on which the new State was founded. But for the hardest hard core of their membership this affiliation went too far. In Jerusalem at some time in the earlier years of the war, perhaps about 1942, there emerged from the turbulent floods of those years, clinging to its rock of faith and salvation, a small body calling itself Neturei Karta, the Guardians of the City. It was content to remain outside 'history', to have no truck either with the Zionist Satan or with its own ex-colleagues in Agudat Israel, and to sacrifice everything else in order to safeguard the essential. The world has heard of it since, and we shall deal with it again.

In the realm of practical politics after the end of the world war, and before the Arab countries made their all-out attacks on the embryo new State, there were thus three distinct political elements. One was

embattled nationalism. Its military arms were the citizen army of the ①
Hagana and the terrorist groups fighting both Arabs and British; its
political arm was the Jewish Agency, the Zionist body containing
members of a shadow government ready for the end of the visibly
expiring British mandate. The second was the bulk of the orthodox ②
religious community with the Rabbinate at its head, at one with the
nationalists in the drive for independence but determined to maintain
its own position, with the help of its political instrument, the Mizrachi
party. The third element was Agudat Israel, opposed to the Zionist ③
philosophy and with reservations about any secular government, but
ready to accept the logic of events to the extent of helping to safeguard
the future of the people, so long as this did not mean sacrificing the
religious principles which alone gave that future a meaning. The
ideological gulfs were wide but it was essential to reach some understanding among the three. Nothing but effective national unity could
save the Jewish community from the many dangers that pressed upon
it. After some very hard bargaining an agreement was hammered out.
It was embodied in a letter to Aguda, dated 19 June 1947 and signed on
behalf of all sections of the Zionist Coalition – by Ben-Gurion as head
of the Agency, J. L. Fishman of the Mizrachi party, and the General
Zionist representative, Greenbaum. The following are the material
parts of the letter:[8]

(a) *Sabbath*. It is clear that the legal day of rest in the Jewish State
should be the Sabbath, with Christians and members of other
faiths naturally being granted the right to rest on their own festive
day of the week.
(b) *Dietary laws*. All necessary measures should be taken to guarantee
that in every State Kitchen intended for Jews the food will be Kosher.
(c) *Marriage*. All members of the Executive appreciate the gravity
of the problem and its great difficulties, and on the part of all
bodies represented by the Executive of the Agency everything
possible will be done to satisfy in this respect the profound need of
adherents of the faith, so as to prevent the division of the House of
Israel into two parts.
(d) *Education*. The full autonomy of every 'trend'[9] in education
will be guaranteed . . . there will be no interference on the part of
the Government with the religious conviction and the religious
conscience of any section in Israel. The State will naturally
determine minimal compulsory studies, the Hebrew language,

history, sciences etc., and supervise the fulfilment of this minimum, but it will give full freedom to every 'trend' to conduct education according to its own conviction and will refrain from any interference with religious conscience.

This was forthright enough. The paragraph dealing with marriage meant more than it needed to say. Under the Mandate, the Government had dealt with the Jewish community as a sort of club, with individual right of entry and withdrawal. The writ of the Rabbinate over personal law, including marriage and divorce, ran up to the limits of the Jewish community. But these were set by the voluntary choice of its individual members. In the Jewish State there could be no right of entry or withdrawal for any Jewish citizen, as he would then be. His position would be defined by objective legal standards. So if the authority of the Rabbinate in the sphere of personal law was to continue, the Rabbinical Courts must be entrenched as part of the judicial apparatus of the State itself, and their writ must run throughout the Jewish community, whatever its individual members' views.

All this was to apply in what was to be, by definition, a secular State based on religious freedom. It was an odd bargain and a one-sided one. Ben-Gurion, who first adumbrated the 'compromise' and then as Prime Minister enacted it, has been frank about his reasons.

I knew that we required the widest possible political backing to carry out the gigantic tasks that I envisaged . . . the wider the coalition the narrower would be the list of policy items on which I would get general agreement. I was prepared to limit my programme to the basic urgencies and offer concessions on what I regarded as subsidiary issues.[10]

There was at some early stage a specific argument about whether the dietary laws were to be applied in the army. 'Kosher Kitchens to them [the religious parties] were of paramount importance; to me they were of subsidiary interest . . . moreover serving soldiers who were religious had the right to Kosher food.'[11] There it all is in a nutshell. Sharp though the differences in conviction were, it was unthinkable that the Jewish State should compel an orthodox Jewish minority to give up what its beliefs held vital. The secular majority must yield on what to its free-thinking mind could only be, as Ben-Gurion said, subsidiary. So the new State entered on its course not only ringed by implacable enemies but founded on an internal agreement which was fundamental to its life yet inherently unstable. It represented no real consensus, and concealed differences which could well break out into a disruptive conflict of radically opposed convictions. Both abroad and at home, dragons' teeth had been sown.

To quit at that point the story of Palestine up to the foundation of the State of Israel would be to say nothing about the external setting in which it must live its life. The obverse of the Zionist medal bore an image of a different kind. The two most profound of the Zionist thinkers themselves realized this, and in passages of their writings which are either unknown or neglected, they said so.

The land to which the Jews for so long turned their faces had for a millennium and a quarter been inhabited mainly by another Semitic people, the descendants of those Arabs who had overrun it in the explosive aftermath of Mahomet's life. They had been misgoverned for centuries by the Turks and at the time of the early Jewish settlements, and for long before these, they were scratching a subsistence from neglected soil, paying heavy tribute to their Arab landlords and Turkish governors. Their ideas and interests did not go beyond the life of their families and their villages. The modern world of material progress and assertive nationalism had not touched them.

From that point the story can be taken up in the words of Ahad Ha'am,[12] who in 1891 – six years before the publication of Herzl's manifesto – wrote an article called 'The Truth from Palestine'. These are extracts:

We abroad are accustomed to believe that the Arabs are all savages who are living on the level of animals, and who do not understand what is happening here around them. This, however, is a great mistake. The Arab, like all Semites, possesses a sharp intelligence and great cunning. The Arabs, and particularly the urban population, see through our activity in the country and its purpose but they keep silent, since for the time being they do not fear any danger for their future. When, however, the life of our people in Palestine will have developed to such an extent that the indigenous population will feel threatened, then they will not easily give way any longer.

How careful must we be in dealing with an alien people in whose midst we want to settle. How essential is it to practise kindness and esteem towards them . . . For if ever the Arab could consider the action of his rivals to be oppression or the robbing of his rights then, even if he keeps silent and waits for his time to come, the rage will remain alive in his heart.

The academic theory was equally high-minded. Martin Buber submitted to the Zionist Congress in Carlsbad in 1921 a resolution which it adopted: 'It is our fervent wish to live in peace and fraternity with the Arabs of Palestine, and to build with them a flourishing Commonwealth, which will enable the two communities to create their own national lives.'

But only the year before, with the evidences of Zionist policy around him, Ahad Ha'am had written the bitter words: 'Since the beginning of the Palestinian colonisation we have always considered the Arab people as non-existent.' The criticism was echoed a generation later in the Report of the Anglo-American Committee of 1946:

> It is not unfair to say that the Jewish community in Palestine has never, as a community, faced the problem of co-operation with the Arabs. It is significant that in the Jewish Agency's proposal for a Jewish State, the problem of handling a million and a quarter Arabs is dealt with in the vaguest generalities.

Here are two further quotations, from Aaron David Gordon, who like Ahad Ha'am believed relations with the Arabs to be crucial. 'Our attitude towards them must be one of humanity, of moral courage which remains on the highest plane even if the behaviour of the other side is not all that is desired. Indeed their hostility is all the more a reason for our humanity.' In 1922 he included, in statutes he drew up for the guidance of settlements, this clause:

> Wherever settlements are founded, a specific share of the land must be assigned to the Arabs from the outset. The distribution of sites should be equitable so that not only the welfare of the Jewish settlers but equally that of the resident Arabs will be safeguarded. The settlement has the moral obligation to assist the Arabs in any way it can. This is the only proper and fruitful way to establish good neighbourly relations with the Arabs.[13]

These challenges remained to confront the new State, and in a later chapter we shall examine the response.

Division

3

'Who is a Jew?'

the constit'l foundation

In the Museum of Modern Art in Tel Aviv, before a special meeting of the National Council, on 14 May 1948, David Ben-Gurion proclaimed the State of Israel. It was to be a secular state but among its historic memories was the gift to the world by that people in that Land of 'the eternal Book of Books', and its foundations were to be 'liberty, justice and peace as envisioned by the Prophets of Israel'. It would guarantee freedom of religion and conscience.

The drafting had presented considerable difficulty. It took several days before the secular and religious could agree on the reference to the Almighty, who made only one concluding appearance, dubiously veiled as the 'Rock of Israel'. It must have seemed, to the four rabbis who were among the signatories, a grudging acknowledgment by the People of the eternal Book of Books of that God whose prophets were providing the foundations of the newly proclaimed state. They may, however, have remembered with some satisfaction, as they listened to the reference to religious freedom, that the letter of nearly a year earlier (p. 29) had ensured a strictly halachic construction of the phrase.

In fact the public life of the State has never for long been free of dispute on the subject. It will throw light on the general background if we begin with the sharp argument that developed in 1950 about whether there should be a written constitution, enshrining the values on which the State was founded. To a country like Britain, which preserves its national *ethos* unconfined by verbal forms, this might not seem necessary. But even in Britain the relation of Church and State has what amounts to constitutional embodiment. How much more would the idea appeal to political leaders with no tradition of flexible responsibility in government, but schooled in a positive conception of Statehood either by Hegel (via Marx) or by the assumptions of Russian centralism or of course by that universal *vade mecum* the Torah itself.

The difficulty was that while one group would accept no written embodiment of values other than those of the Torah, the other talked about the spirit of the early socialist pioneers, the spirit of the ingathering, and so on. The end was an agreement to differ, the alternative being to tear apart the fabric of the young state by an argument that would go dangerously near the roots of its being. This deeply felt division of approach showed itself again and again. Sometimes the matters in dispute could have been treated as technical and settled without difficulty, on that basis. But they never were: like two litigious neighbours, the combatants could not restrain themselves from taking to court issues which in another atmosphere might have been disposed of by a few friendly words over the fence.

The most obtrusive problems were those affecting public observance, covered by the first two of the four key paragraphs in the letter of agreement. Keeping the Sabbath and the Jewish festivals roused no great opposition: even the 'secular' acknowledged the value of the 'orders of Rule and Law'; few were ready to abandon practices at once so time-honoured, so characteristic of Jewish life, and on the whole so sensible. There have however been arguments, sometimes bitter, over the dispensations the Minister for Labour may grant on practical grounds – the needs of defence, of the national economy, of essential public services, of security of life and property. There is specific precedent in the halacha for such departures (Jesus was appealing to one when he spoke of the right to rescue on the Sabbath an animal fallen into a pit) but the Minister's discretion was likely to be, and often has been, questioned by those of stricter outlook. The whole situation as an observer sees it is extremely untidy: one effect of religious law is to compel the Tel-Aviv citizen to travel on the Sabbath more expensively by group taxi than he could by bus. Private traffic on the Sabbath is not banned, public transport is – if the municipality so decides. Buses run in Haifa, cafés open in Tel-Aviv, Jerusalem forgoes both.

When issues take a new form, however, they can be explosive. Late in 1969 the whole country was torn apart over the question whether TV was to be permitted on the Sabbath. By a typical arrangement between the National Religious Party and the Government, it was to be banned, in disregard of a pledge made at the then very recent election. The ban took the form of a 'request' from the Prime Minister which however the Broadcasting Authority decided to reject: it did so by a majority vote and the religious minority appealed to the Prime Minister who allowed the appeal. Then, after a series of politico-legal manoeuvres which might have seemed a caricature had they appeared in a political stage-skit, Sabbath TV finally won the day, to the undisguised pleasure of most of the public.[1] (It has been remarked incidentally that Sabbath radio bequeathed by the Christian Mandatory power has been accepted as part of the natural order of things, while Sabbath TV, the act of a Jewish government, was perhaps for that very reason a stone of stumbling and a rock of offence.)

The imposition of orthodox dietary law on hotels and restaurants, under the sanction of a refusal by the Rabbinate to grant them a certificate of correctness, is now accepted quietly. American tourists, even lax ones, are known to like to find ancestral practices in vogue in the Jewish State, and in any case exceptions can and do exist, since the certificate is not always a necessary condition of commercial success. Again the ban on pig-rearing, except for a predominantly Christian area around Nazareth, causes no resentment, since the objection to eating pig-meat is not confined to the orthodox: pig to most seculars is, for not entirely different reasons, like horsemeat to an Englishman – not forbidden, merely under an emotional tabu. On the whole the dietary laws are not an inflammatory issue, though there was a world-famous argument, which the Rabbinate won, about the serving of non-Kosher food in the State steamship line, and another, which they lost, when they tried to prevent the opening of a large, efficient and ritually correct slaughterhouse which would compete with smaller and more backward ones.

It is when we turn to the exercise of rabbinical authority and the imposition of halachic law in the spheres of marriage and divorce, and of Jewish nationality, that the truly serious problems arise. The first and most pervasive effect is that in Israel there is no civil marriage: those not married by an orthodox rabbi according to the halacha (for example, a Christian to a Jewish partner, or a 'Cohen', with his priestly ancestry, to a divorced woman) are not legally married. If they live together without ceremony, in a 'common law marriage' which is recognized under the traditional law, their children have no Jewish status and may face considerable difficulties in getting married when their time comes. The same problem awaits, on their maturity, the children of a couple who may have (as some do) flown to Cyprus to be married in defiance of halachic rules, or to America, as did one Supreme Court judge.

Difficulties of another kind may arise if the widow of a man lost at sea wishes to remarry: she cannot furnish such proof of death as the halacha requires. Again, a childless widow with unmarried brothers-in-law may not remarry unless they renounce their prior claim: or she may in certain circumstances find it impossible to establish the death of the brother-in-law where this would leave her free. These are infrequent cases but they do occur, and are fuel to the flames of secular indignation.

On the other hand, to tamper with the existing situation would deeply affect the unity of the State itself. This to many secular citizens is the fundamental difficulty. It explains why a number of non-religious members of the Knesset originally voted for the relevant Act, the Marriage and Divorce Law. Since an orthodox Jew could not marry (for example) the child of a Jewish father and gentile mother, the alternative to the present imposition of orthodox law on the secular would soon be the development of two mutually exclusive, non-intermarrying Jewish communities within the State.

The fact that the position of Jews in the Diaspora would be affected since the cleavage between the two types of marital regime would be world-wide, is a point that troubles religious Jews perhaps more than the secular. In any case the position is complex, since a large fraction of the vast American Jewish community does not – in the eyes of the orthodox – live under halachic law and marriages performed by its rabbis would not be acceptable to the Rabbinate in Israel. This is referred to below.

The most important political result of the halachic view of marriage is to be seen in its effect on the problem of Jewish nationality: it is in fact one of the roots of the now world-famous question 'Who is a Jew?' So too are some other factors, as was shown by the famous Rufeisen case of 1950, which of all nationality issues raised the loudest and longest echoes, at least until the Schalit case of 1969–70 to which we shall be turning.

Oswald Rufeisen was a Polish Jew, a brave anti-Nazi resistance fighter, who took refuge in a monastery, became converted and took Orders as a Carmelite monk. But he still felt himself to be Jew enough to want to return to Israel to live and work. He claimed the right of entry under the Law of Return, i.e. as a recognized Jew. The authorities refused him entry under that Law, and he appealed to the Courts. Under halachic law he was without question a Jew, born of a Jewish mother. The tradition was 'once a Jew, always a Jew': you could be a wicked Jew, a deserting Jew, a treacherous Jew, but a Jew you remained. The authorities were constantly and without question admitting under the Law of Return atheists with Jewish mothers.

The Supreme Court ruled, by majority, that since the Law of Return contained no definition of 'Jew', ordinary usage, 'the language of men' must be the governing factor. Under that usage, the term was commonly applied to many who did not adhere to or practise Judaism, but never to anyone who had voluntarily adopted another faith. To call a Christian a Jew would be to rob historic Jewish tradition of its meaning. In effect, halachic law must bow before the Jewish people's present idea of its own identity.

This would appear to carry two startling implications. After two thousand years in which the Law in all its strictness had been the binding force holding Jewry together, the Jewish State through its judiciary had decided to supersede it. Secondly, and fraught with even greater significance for the future, the new determining factor was both vague and impermanent. Vague – because what precise meaning can one give to the self-identification of a people whose attitudes to the religion which had shaped it were now varied enough to embrace as a majority view a combination of indifference and hostility? Impermanent, because while the Jewish people's idea of itself might be clear-cut and beyond question in 1958, and for as many more years as anyone could foresee, it could change. Indeed under the precedents of history it was far more likely to change than not. An exception to the precedent of change had been the Jewish people itself – but what became now of even that exception?

To dwell on this a moment longer: perhaps the most profound of all the questions one might ask about Judaism is whether it transcends history or is created by it. This is no academic issue: it goes to the root of the problem of Jewish identity. The Rufeisen judgment appears to range the official panoply of the Jewish State firmly against the transcendental and with the historical or existentialist conception of Judaism. The consequences are bound to be significant and some began to appear before many years.

To clear the ground for an attempt to justify that statement, we will go back once more to 1958, the year not only of Rufeisen but of one of the most noted of several disputes arising out of the system of registration. It is a duty of the Ministry of the Interior to register all citizens, under classifying marks, one of which is 'ethnic affiliation'. The vagueness of this category had been leading to a wide range of interpretation by the officials on the spot. The Minister of the day issued regulations to the effect that anyone who called himself a Jew and did not belong to another faith was to be registered as one, and that the religion (or 'ethnic affiliation') of children was to be registered in accordance with the parents' wish. The religious ministers resigned from the Government, since this regulation could well have meant contravening halachic law by registering as Jewish the children of a gentile mother, if she and the (presumably Jewish) father so wished. Here was direct confrontation: did the Jewish State determine Jewishness as any other State lays down the criteria of its citizenship, or was Jewishness determined by the halacha, something anterior to the State and beyond its jurisdiction? Mr Menachem Beigin, the former head of the 'terrorist' faction Irgun Zwei Le'umi in the War of Independence, asked in the Knesset 'Who empowered any government or any elected body in Israel to determine who was a Jew?' Mr Ben-Gurion, the Prime Minister, referred the issue to forty-three rabbis and scholars for their comment: remembering – a little late in the day – that it was of interest beyond the confines of the State, he included a number of leaders in the Diaspora among his referees. The replies indicated a very large majority, including most of the secular scholars, against the Government's policy. The final compromise, in 1960, avoided registering a child as Jewish in possible breach of traditional law, by laying it down that a minor's religion was not determined until he was of age and could declare it himself. The religious Ministers returned.

It was about a decade before the registration system in relation to the marriage laws was again involved and the implications, and consequences, were even more far-reaching. This was the case of Benjamin Schalit, a naval officer with a Scottish wife whom he had met and married in Edinburgh. Though not, apparently, a believing Christian she refused on grounds of principle to take the common course of becoming a Jewish convert in order to avoid subsequent difficulties for her two children. After 1958 the Ministry of the Interior had been allotted under Coalition Government arrangements to the Religious Party, and the Minister had subsequently laid it down for the first time that his officials were not to register as Jewish, children who were not so under halachic law – as clearly the Schalit boy and girl were not. The space under the heading of ethnic affiliation was to be left blank. This refusal the father challenged, and took the issue to Court. It was remitted to the High Court which after deliberating for eighteen months delivered judgment in January 1970.[2]

The nine members of the Court decided by five against four, the minority including the President, that the plaintiff was entitled to his case. The judgments were delivered individually and all but one were reasoned arguments. The substance of the majority view was as follows: the determination of Jewish status is an ideological issue of profound importance, touching not only the foundations of the Jewish State but the position of Jews everywhere in the world. It was not however an issue capable of judicial decision, since the term 'Jew' has no fixed and immutable meaning and can be given only a limited definition related to the particular purpose of the relevant legislative Act. In this instance, the process of registration was carried out for administrative purposes, largely statistical, and the law must be construed in that context. The only issue the Court was qualified to settle was whether the registering officer had acted correctly in following his Minister's directive – or whether the Minister was using his powers properly in issuing it – that the children of a mixed marriage shall have their ethnic affiliation entry left blank. The administrative purposes of registration were not rightly served by introducing the external consideration of whether a marriage was validly Jewish under religious law – a consideration which had no place in the decisions of a secular court: the officer's duty was to enter what the parents told him to unless it was on the face of it absurdly untrue.

It must be noted, and might seem to lend some general support to the majority view, that the law says explicitly both that the entries on a registration card cannot be taken as *prima facie* evidence of their correctness, and also that they are of no effect in relation to the laws which lay down rules for marriage and divorce. Here, the halachic code prevails, whatever a registration card may say; to enter the Schalit children as Jewish would not make them so if and when they wished to marry a Jewish partner under religious law. To some Israeli lawyers and others it seemed that the case for treating the issue as technical, and not one of fundamental principle, was overwhelming. But this was one more instance where the real underlying issue was not to be suppressed. Four of the judges insisted on penetrating what they saw as the technical and legal façade and dealing with the essence of the matter. It would be an evasion, they felt, not to deal with the 'awesome and weighty issue' whether ethnic and religious affiliation can be separated: whether the immemorially hallowed identification of Jewish nationality and Jewish religion was to be split apart, in the name of some contemporary disposition to identify Jewishness with 'Jewish-Israeli culture' – as the plaintiff had explicitly demanded.

One might have expected the division of judicial opinion to follow the boundary line between religious and secular atttiudes on the bench. But this was not so. One of the weightiest pronouncements came from Mr Justice Silberg. This judge's formulation of the reason for refusing entry to Rufeisen had had considerable public impact, and he devoted part of his Schalit judgment to setting out the difference between the two as he saw it. The Law of Return, governing the Rufeisen case, talks the language of the ordinary man, to whom a Christian cannot be a Jew. In the Registration Act the term Jew was not used; and for a definition of 'ethnic group' one could turn in the case of a Jew nowhere but to the halacha. Justice Silberg's general position was described, in the judgment of one of his colleagues, as that of a non-observant Jew who nevertheless recognized the power and significance of tradition, of the idea that people and religion were identical, of the halacha itself as an irreplaceable constituent in and asset to the life of the Jewish people. He himself dismissed the possibility of identifying Jewishness with Jewish-Israeli culture and values on three grounds: that the Jewish nation is wider than Israel; that there is no such Jewish-Israeli nationality yet established in Israel amid the present flux of ideas and attitudes; and that even if there were, religious ideas were too strongly held among religious intellectuals, and were making too much appeal to the younger generation of seculars, to permit any identification of such a national spirit with secular attitudes. His concluding remarks made plain his opinion that the search for a new test for national identity would constitute an absolute denial of the continued existence of the Jewish people, and that the aspiration to build a new Levantine nation, without past or tradition, was in conflict with the purposes for which the great task of spreading the doctrine of Zionism had been undertaken.

Whatever the legal merit of the case for regarding the Schalit issue as technical, it was clear that the minority of four who refused to do so were more nearly in tune with the political sentiments and instincts of the public. The judgment itself precipitated a fierce argument, which threatened – even with the Arabs at the gates – to split public opinion, Knesset membership and the Government itself. Chief Rabbi Unterman attacked the decision as 'rooting out a cornerstone of Judaism which has preserved the purity of the Jewish family from all incursions of foreign culture and miscegenation'. The Minister for Religious Affairs declared, 'We shall not live by the dictates of the Court'. The Rabbinate's chief executive, at a religious service at its headquarters, adopted the recognized emergency procedure of delaying the reading of the Law to complain 'before the congregation and God' of an injustice. It is true that the 'seculars' saw it differently. The *Jerusalem Post* expected the tumult to die down when it was realized that the halachic definition of Jewry was untouched. A Rabbi of American origin saw the moral of the situation as a need to replace the old conception of Jewish identity with new forms, and a new synthesis embodied in a new and more 'pluralist' framework of religious institutions. The Professor of Sociology at the Hebrew University agreed that the time for a pluralist approach had come, and thought it a better way of dealing with sharp differences of opinion than by political bargaining between the contenders. The future criterion of Jewishness in his view could only be acceptance of and participation in a way of life as lived by the Jewish people in its land. 'The crucial test,' he said, 'is when we feel the common bond stronger than anything else.'

But this, as the outbursts from the religious camp showed, was a long way from practical politics. Clearly something had to be done if serious social disruption was to be avoided. There were protests from those who thought it improper to tamper by political action with judicial findings – protests which did not suggest any great knowledge of the practices of governments in older democracies when confronted by legal interpretations unacceptable to current sentiment among the public or in the legislature. In spite of such protests, an understanding was in fact hammered out between the opposing groups and the Government embodied it in a substantial amendment to the Law of Return presented to the Knesset in March 1970. The Bill reinstated the halachic criterion of Jewish 'ethnic affiliation' for the purpose of registration, so that the 'religion' of children of mixed marriages would not be settled for them by their parents: on the other hand the Law of Return would be amended to grant automatic citizenship rights to the gentile spouses and adult descendants of those eligible for entry, down to the third generation, and even if the man or woman whose own Jewish status was the basis of these new rights were no longer alive. Citizenship rights carry important civil and fiscal advantages but do not change their possessor's status under religious law. The gentile wife of a returning Jew would enter as an Israeli citizen but neither she nor her children would be recognized as Jewish (except by conversion). The same rights could be applied for by those already resident, but their acquisition was not automatic.

If the success of a political bargain is to be measured by the apparent conviction with which both sides claim to have got what they wanted, this one must take a high rank. The religious did not doubt their victory: the halachic conception of Jewish identity by descent or conversion was preserved. (The fact that it had been breached eleven years earlier in the Rufeisen case was not allowed to mar the rejoicing.) The secular felt that they had been relieved of a rankling grievance which imposed not only religious but civil disabilities on non-Jewish partners and their descendants. They appreciated particularly the fact that if and when the entry of Russian Jews is allowed by the Soviet government – a cherished hope in Israel – their entry would not be impeded on religious grounds, so long as they had evidence of Jewish blood, and despite the doubts about their religious status raised by the halachic uncertainties attending their Russian lives. This particular argument played a distinct part in persuading a number of secular members of the Knesset to accept the reversal of the Schalit judgment. The 'seculars' took some satisfaction, too, in the fact that agreement had been reached, and a dangerous national split averted. While this hardly counts as a score for their side, it helps to account for their readiness to accept the bargain. Whether this should be reckoned a strength or a weakness on their part is a moot point.

There was however one point of great doctrinal and practical significance left open. The manner of the conversion was not specified. Under the amended law an immigrant who has a certificate of conversion to Judaism provided by any Jewish community in the world will not only receive full citizenship rights but be registered as a Jew. This means that the State, since it refuses to distinguish between various Jewish religious groupings abroad, recognizes as valid under its own legislation conversions effected by non-orthodox rabbis, including rabbis of the Reform and Conservative movements in the USA who between them outnumber the orthodox by about two to one. When the Minister of Justice spoke of this to the Knesset he added pointedly, 'However, in matters of marriage the State is not the master'. It could in other words not prevent the Rabbinate refusing to recognize as Jewish, for the purpose of marriage, a convert whom the State had registered as Jewish. This appeared at the time to leave the orthodox content – they did not protest and professed themselves satisfied that the *status quo* was unaltered. The leader of the Agudat Israel party in the Knesset, however, expressed in the usual emphatic terms his fears that the absence of any definition of conversion would lead not only to the admittance as Jews (by religion) of immigrants not validly married, but also to the recognition of Reform rabbis in Israel itself and ultimately, on both counts, to the growth in Israel of two kinds of Jews,

real Jews under the Marriage and Divorce Law, pseudo-Jews invalidly
wedded abroad and even at home. After a generation or two proof of
status would become impossible. Everyone would have to keep a
detailed family tree. 'People will have to realise that a document
testifying to the Jewishness of a person hailing from Israel will not be
worthy of belief.'

This was in March 1970. Towards the end of May the question of the
validity of conversion by Reform rabbis in Israel was brought to the
front by the case of a Christian lady converted by a 'progressive'
Jewish rabbi in Tel Aviv. Apparently under legal advice from militant
seculars she brought a High Court action designed to establish her
right to registration as a Jewess. The National Religious Party's
Executive decided to 'stop sharing responsibility for the Government'
unless Reform conversions were prohibited, and in not unfamiliar
fashion the doctrinal imbroglio became a political crisis. The Chief
Rabbinate early in June (that is, nearly three months after the passing
of the new law) declared officially that it would 'shake the foundations
of the House of Israel and result in a schism the like of which has not
been seen since the break up of the Jewish nation into two Kingdoms'
(i.e. after the death of King Solomon). It also declared flatly that any
non-halachic conversion, whether in Israel or abroad, was not considered to be a conversion. The Government then reaffirmed its general
adherence to the *status quo* agreement. The Minister of Justice, in a
published letter to the Minister for the Interior, distinguished between
the positions abroad, where the Government of Israel could not draw
dividing lines between the halachic authority of various denominations,
and in Israel, where the Mandatory Government ordinance of 1927 still
applied, and the Rabbinate as head of the religious community enjoyed
sole recognition for the making of conversions. The letter affirmed the
view that a refusal by the Minister of the Interior to register as Jewish
anyone converted in Israel by a Reform rabbi would be lawful, and
declared that this position would be defended in the Courts.

Meantime the ex-Christian lady's marriage was legally valid, and
her registration as Jewish a possibility. This was in direct contradiction
to the policy of the Government, and with it the *status quo* and the
basis of the coalition with the religious parties. Something had to be
done. Another legislative reversal of a possible Court decision was
unthinkable. In this cliff-hanging situation the rescuer appeared wearing,
in the best style of old-time melodrama, a military uniform. The
lady was persuaded to apply to be converted once again, in orthodox

fashion, and the Chief Rabbi to the Israeli Armed Forces, having satisfied himself of the applicant's bona fides, carried out what a newspaper termed 'a *blitz* conversion', done in a few hours (the orthodox procedures normally take about a year from first to last) in his office, before a rabbinical court consisting of himself and two army rabbis. The Chief Rabbi was reported to have based himself on a saying of Maimonides: 'One should not be too cumbersome and should not be too exact on occasion, lest one should create a burden and lead a man to deviate from good to bad ways.' It was suggested publicly that Maimonides' ally had been Defence Minister Dayan, who is not entirely inexperienced in the use of sudden military sorties to avoid anything cumbersome or over-exact. It was also said in terms by the *Jerusalem Post* that the considerable pressure to which the Government had been subjected included the influence of the President of the State who, as a fervent Habad Hasid, allowed himself to be part of the Habad campaign against Reform conversion conducted from across the Atlantic at the behest of the Lubavitsche Rebbe (a second spiritual leader of ultra-orthodox groups in Israel, operating from America).

There are several reasons why this episode deserves to be recorded in more permanent form than the pages of the daily press (which did it full justice). It has that larger-than-life quality that marks so many politico-religious crises in Israel. It indicates better than pages of generalization how the complexities of politics in a secular state which is partially under religious authority are apt to be worked out. Even more typically and significantly, it had an obvious *ad hoc* quality. It settled nothing beyond the particular case, and so reflected faithfully the indeterminate condition of the entire 'Who is a Jew' situation, as the amended Law of Return has left it. The religious party leader who foresaw trouble in maintaining the halachic purity of the religious community in Israel surely had a point, and the continued refusal to recognize Reform rabbis in Israel does not meet it.

The civil rights newly conferred on non-Jews may lead to the development of a section of Israeli society living in the closest association with Jews but not technically Jewish. May this not come to involve just that communal division whose avoidance has been put forward as one of the main arguments against civil marriage? Or, to put the doubt in terms of legal principle rather than practice, does not the new situation mean that there is now a second definition of 'Who is a Jew?'? One, under the Registration Law, is halachic; the other, under the amended Law of Return, is not. Strictly speaking, those de-

fined by the second method are not necessarily Jews. But how long
will it be before the distinction begins to be overlooked by many of
the Israeli public? And how long after that can halachic distinctions
between two types of Israeli citizen, both with Jewish links, be preserved? Nor is that all.

Some immigrants who have been married or converted abroad by
non-orthodox rabbis may have to face, or see their children face, painful
personal situations as the result of the Rabbinate's attitude, and the
Government's inability to frustrate it by breaching the *status quo*. But
the Government is also without power to impose orthodox procedures
on Reform and Conservative communities abroad. It certainly lacks
the will to alienate powerful American friends, and so is in a dilemma
that is already embarrassing and could become dangerous. It may be,
as orthodox believers claim, that the great bulk of American immigrants are from the ranks of those who are faithful to the Tradition
and are therefore Israel's only committed allies. The fact remains that
about two thirds of the vast American community are not orthodox.
They provide some migrants, but also furnish a great deal of material
support, have an impact on the American political scene, and though
they do not normally (as do some sections of the orthodox) attempt
backstage influence on the domestic affairs of Israel, they are an
important factor in the affairs of the State. Their loyalty may not be
proof indefinitely against the strains put upon it by the intransigent
policies of the Rabbinate. The Reform community numbers about a
million and a quarter in America, not to mention the 30,000 Reform
and Liberal Jews in Britain. A rabbi of that community holding
representative positions both in America and Israel, (where he was
temporarily resident) wrote as follows two weeks after the 'resolution'
of the conversion crisis:

Ever since the debate over 'Who is a Jew' the rabbinate and the
National Religious Party have been vehemently opposing Reform
conversion . . . And now, after months of slander of Reform
Judaism and its leaders, they themselves take a convert prepared by
a Reform Rabbi, who is married to a Cohen, who lives at a
kibbutz where neither Kashrut nor Shabbat is observed, and
convert her in a flash . . . It is not the desire to preserve the
Halacha which motivates the Orthodox Rabbinate, but rather the
desire to keep the Halacha as their special preserve . . . They know
that there is no logical reason for sanctioning conversions by

Reform rabbis abroad and for denying the right of these same rabbis to convert once they have settled in Israel. And so, recognizing that both time and logic were against them, they decided to exploit the delicate political situation in order to strengthen their monopoly over religious life. In so doing they employed old-fashioned political blackmail clothed in the garb of religion. Their stated purpose was to unify the Jewish people. But the consequence of their action was to divide the Jewish people and to threaten to dissolve the coalition government at the very time when solidarity is so essential to the well-being of both the State and the people . . . To maintain that the Jews of America want the Orthodox Religious Party to have a monopoly over Jewish religious life in Israel is ludicrous, as well as untrue. What is true, unfortunately, is that a small minority of American Orthodox Jews, who have continuously failed in their efforts to diminish the influence of Conservative and Reform Judaism in America, now see in the State of Israel a political instrument for imposing a second-class status on non-Orthodox Jews.[3]

The unbridled language and unqualified ascription of base motives, presumably not common in the Rabbi's American environment, are not wholly out of line with the native style of 'religious' controversy in Israel. But the bitterness revealed, and the deep seated differences of approach, throw a lurid light on the background not only of life in Israel but of the Israel-Diaspora relations with which a later chapter is concerned.

4

Segregation in the Schools

In the perspective of history the most significant aspect of the division between orthodox and secular attitudes is likely to be its effect in the schools: here the division becomes self-perpetuating, indeed on present evidence self-aggravating.

The Jewish educational system had its origins well back under Turkish rule, to which it owed nothing. Its inspiration was from Jewish organizations abroad, in Britain, France, Germany, Austria and Russia: on the spot, an important influence was that of the Teachers' Association which took a positive interest in the pattern of education and classroom curricula. Under the Mandatory Government, first the Zionist movement, then the Jewish National Council, were in charge and managed – without substantial help from the Government and with no powers to compel attendance – to provide an elementary education for the great majority of Jewish children. Outside this were the ultra-orthodox system on one hand, and on the other the Kibbutzim which furnished their own offspring with a full range of primary and secondary education.

The split between the religious and secular systems went still further. Apart from the ultra-orthodox and within the autonomous Jewish system itself, the usual partisan approach resulted in the usual divided pattern. There were besides Aguda, three sets of schools run respectively by the Mizrachi (religious Zionist) party, the Histadrut, representing the secular labour view, and a third 'General Zionist' influence. Under *originally* broad central supervision each of them had considerable freedom to *four* shape its own educational policies and curricula in accordance with its *systems* own outlook and philosophy. This pattern persisted until the foundation of the State, when the Education Act of 1949 recognized not only the three named trends but also the Agudat Israel (ultra-orthodox) schools, and left each of the four under the control of its sponsor, largely independent of central authority.

49

This worked out badly. The party sponsors used their strength and influence to attract or (in effect) compel any parents they could reach to send their children to one of their schools. Competition became more intense when the big flow of oriental immigrants began. The Labour trend set up within its own system a religious sub-division, to avoid the otherwise foregone conclusion that orthodox Jews from Africa or the Yemen – such of them as understood what they were doing – would send their children elsewhere. Immigrants on settlements were bargained over, *en bloc*, and their children sometimes allotted to the 'trend' of the political party in control of their settlement regardless of its suitability to their ideas. Some of the methods used were scandalous and there was in fact open scandal. An Education Minister resigned, before long the Coalition broke apart, the Government resigned and went to the country (1951). For the sake of national unity and in fairness to the new immigrants, change was essential. After two years of bargaining and manoeuvre, education was transferred in 1953 to the control of the State, with affiliation to outside bodies expressly barred.

The Act laid down its terms of reference for the new system. It was to inculcate 'the values of Jewish culture and the achievements of science . . . love of the homeland and loyalty to the State and the Jewish people'. There were explicit references to the old ideology of land work and handcraft, and a definition of 'society built on freedom, equality, tolerance, mutual assistance, and love of mankind. This wording was tailored to the needs of the secular, nationalist 'ol'd-line' Zionist; nothing in it could upset the most doctrinaire of Jewish atheists. But a choice was offered between 'State' and 'Religious State' schools, the latter set apart as 'religious in way of life, curriculum, teachers and inspectors'. There was a further option open to the ultra-orthodox: the Agudat Israel schools, nominally outside the State system, were 'recognized'; they could and do receive State subsidies in return for their acceptance of minimum standards, and a degree of light supervision which in practice amounts to self-regulation. The control of the 'religious State' schools, though vested in the Ministry of Education, is also in the hands of a council with a majority of religious sympathizers and almost complete independence in educational policy-making and the choice of staff.

After a few years, the leaders of the State discovered with alarm that many of the pupils in the secular elementary schools, who are a large majority of Israeli children, were in danger of losing or had already lost touch with the traditions of their people. They knew little of the historic festivals and ceremonies, synagogue liturgy meant nothing to them, the history of the Jews in exile bored or repelled them, they increasingly thought of themselves as Israeli citizens, less and less as Jews, and so far from feeling kinship with Jews overseas, were indifferent to or quite often contemptuous of them. This was taking matters a great deal beyond what the older generation, however 'secular', could accept. It came home to them that to rely on Biblical teaching for the inculcation even of national values, let alone religious, was like relying on English history up to Edward the Confessor to convey to an English or American child the spirit and background of his country's life. In 1959, in accordance with a resolution of the Knesset, the Minister of Education prescribed a subject called Jewish Consciousness, aimed at deepening children's understanding of the present relevance of Jewish history and tradition, and their awareness of their heritage and its meaning. One does not find many, in or out of the educational system, who now feel that the attempt has had any very profound success.

Two years after the initiation of the new programme the Ministry of Education issued a history syllabus for primary schools. The aims laid down for teaching in the *secular* schools included the following.[1]

> To foster in the children the notion that the sublime principles of Israel's religion, the vision of Israel's prophets concerning the Messianic era, the Jews' perseverance in the study of the Torah (divine law), the preservation of the unity of their religious ceremonial, their firm belief in Israel's divine Protector, their continuous attachment to their ancestral homeland, and their belief in redemption have endowed our people with the strength to resist all our enemies and to maintain our independence.

To the outside observer this remarkable passage appears to bear little relation to the aims of secular education as set down in the Act. It has even less to the outlook of the average secular young Israeli. A way of life and thought, a set of social and cultural values, not grounded in the life of the home, can hardly be implanted deep in children's minds in a few hours a week by teachers most of whom are apathetic or antagonistic to the whole spirit of the teaching. To inculcate values by which one does not live oneself is not just undesirable, it is in practice impossible.

In the past few years massive episodes in the life of the State have done something to correct the worst features of the earlier situation and to implant or re-integrate the 'Jewish consciousness' of young people. There is little evidence for crediting much of this to an artificial programme in the schools, even if that has done a little to lessen the unfamiliarity of some elements in Jewish tradition and ceremonial. The difficulty lies at the root of the ideological division in Israel: its importance requires further examination of what in fact happens in the schools.

At the outset the Religious State schools and those of Agudat Israel had rather less than a third of all pupils. The influx of orthodox Jews from Africa and Asia has increased that share a very little.[2] The proportion in religious secondary schools, whether academic or vocational (which all have the same sheep-and-goats division), is appreciably lower: about a quarter. It would seem that a number of pupils of religious elementary schools choose, or are compelled by practical considerations, to make a switch when they reach the secondary level. A comparison of the curricula of the two main types of religious schools suggests a reason.

The main difference is the considerable extra time devoted in religious schools to study of 'the sources' – the Bible and Talmud and other Jewish studies. In the seventh and eighth grades – say, thirteen and fourteen-year-olds – of the thirty-two weekly periods, State schools allot four to the Bible, one to the 'oral law', three to Hebrew language and literature – a total of eight, or a quarter of the week's lesson time. Religious State schools give five to the Bible, seven to the oral law, three to language and literature – in all just short of half the total time. The Agudat Israel Schools increase this to eighteen periods out of thirty-two – 56 per cent of lesson time. (Girls in these schools get more Bible, but much less Talmud.) In religious schools the secular subjects that lose some ground to religious teaching are history, geography, the natural sciences and to a smaller extent art, music and 'social education', which last does not figure on the timetable of either type of religious school. Religious parents hold that home is the place for it.

For 'secular' children, one quarter of the weekly timetable might seem a lot to devote to Jewish subjects. Hebrew language and literature can however be taught as a 'secular' subject, like English in Britain or America, and the Bible is taught in a distinctly secular spirit. When it is well and sympathetically taught by a 'secular' teacher it can provide not only a course in national history and culture but something of a liberal education in moral and social values. The author had the opportunity of cross-examining one teacher in a combined elementary and secondary school, brought up himself in a left-wing Kibbutz school, but with a highly professional and responsible attitude to his work. He takes his classes through the principal books of the Old Testament three times, at the ages of about 8–9, 13–14 and 16–17: at first broadly and simply, later more analytically. Many of the narratives are taught as legend but with an underlying meaning. For example, Elijah's confrontation with the prophets of Baal is presented as legend, but the contrast between his more spiritual approach and the pagan rites of self-mutilation is brought out. The depth of the prophetic teaching is exposed: the teacher recalls himself writing an article on what the prophet Amos would have to say today on a street corner in Tel Aviv. Isaiah's passages on the 'suffering servant', which in a religious school would refer to the people of Israel and in a Christian Sunday School to Jesus, is put before these secular children as capable of a variety of interpretations: the prophet himself, the children of Israel, a group of prophetic disciples, Jesus, the exiles in Babylon. When the older children ask about the teacher's own beliefs he tells the truth: if they ask how then he can teach the Bible he explains the value of understanding more deeply the different ways in which it can be interpreted. It is only when he deals with the situation of the Jewish people that he comes a little nearer to indoctrination. He deals with the historic relation between the People and the Land, though without glossing over the fact that it always had other inhabitants: he does not deny that his teaching may well convey the idea of a certain spiritual claim of the People to the Land, an implicit Zionism, but is sure that his teaching is a great deal less nationalist-chauvinist in spirit than in most secular schools. Indeed, other inquiries show that his outlook and methods represent the secular teaching of Bible subjects at its model best, and are well above the average in skill and responsibility. This is not to say that even at a more humdrum level secular Bible teaching has no impact. It could hardly fail to convey something of the meaning of Jewish identity and of the characteristic moral code. As one senior inspector said: it teaches something of Judaism, even if that something hardly goes beyond humanism.

To those professionally engaged on religious education in the religious schools, this outcome of the secular approach was inevitable. From secular teaching, well done, a child (as they see it) may get information, but nothing that will affect his faith or behaviour. Unless the teaching of 'Jewish consciousness' is informed by the spirit of Judaism itself, it cannot increase a child's affection for, or sense of belonging to, the Jewish people. The values of the past are bound to be rejected – as many young Israelis reject them – if the life of the ghetto, for example, is seen as mere passive endurance. Yet to understand the intense spiritual activity that it represented, one must share the sentiment or conviction which inspired and explained it.

There is (to continue the account as one had it from a responsible exponent) a profound contrast between secular humanism and the values by which the exiled Jews lived. Humanism rejects the idea of a demand or command laid on man from without: it seeks its mandate within man himself. It can even accept the religious demand, the need to pray, as something which calls for a response when it makes itself felt in the heart. But in the Jewish religion the religious demand, the duty of prayer, does not begin as an inner felt need but as an unquestionable obligation.

We in the religious schools start with deeds, with observance, in the faith that this will bring us to religion. We pray thrice daily and in the form prescribed, whether we feel like it or not. We are required to create these feelings in ourselves when we pray, we struggle with ourselves to create the need in ourselves.

There is no need to labour the depth of the difference between the two approaches. It is not in itself unique. One finds it exemplified among the members of any civilized society, as individuals. What is peculiar to the situation we are examining is its embodiment in the two parts of a single educational organization, bound in one fellowship of fate (if no other), ready on either part to claim (if anyone seems to question this) that more connects than divides them.

Yet it seems probable that the ideological division in the State must deepen under the influence of two systems of education that differ so radically in their approach to life and the universe. There is distinct evidence, both from common observation and from more systematic inquiry, that most young Israelis resent the time they give to Jewish history in the centuries of dispersion and dislike the substance of it. 'It's all the same, and they never *did* anything', as one young girl athlete put it. But the Hasmonaean warriors and the men of Massada evoke a warm and positive response. Again, while the children of religious upbringing regard Judaism as a complete way of life and make no practical distinction between being a Jew and being an Israeli, the children from partially observant or irreligious homes include a fair-sized minority who see no significant relation between the two and appear to attach no great importance to being of Jewish birth. The tendency is for the pattern of opinion to shift a little in the latter direction. This appears from the facts that more children than parents, or teachers, are of secular outlook (some evidence that home influence is not decisive), and that the oriental immigrants, who tend to be orthodox and provide more than their proportionate share of that category, show distinct signs of assimilating to Western standards in their religious as well as social ideas.

It is much too early to read any of the present signs too dogmatically and the future could have its surprises. But on present appearances the division of the schools seems to be having the result one might expect, in the growth of two kinds of Jew in Israel and a wider gap between them.

The tale of division is not yet complete. Outside the system of general education already described, there is another, wholly orientated towards the traditional teaching and a view of the world limited by its standards. There are two kinds of rabbinical schools: *Talmud Torah*, with 5,000 pupils aged from three to eighteen, and *Yeshivot* (plural of *Yeshiva*), which include both secondary schools and colleges of higher education – the former with a little over 5,000 pupils, the latter with nearly 4,000. This college population is rising. Its total of 4,000 or so compares with a total of about 33,000 undergoing post-secondary education of every kind. *Yeshivot* are of various types, with differences in curriculum, some more 'open' in spirit than others. One can best borrow the description of these bodies given by Joseph Bentwich in his book *Education in Israel*.

Talmud Torah: They still follow the tradition of Jewish education . . . almost unchanged; the content of instruction mainly religious subjects – Bible, Talmud etc. – with only a bare modicum of Hebrew and arithmetic; the language of instruction often Yiddish; the teachers in long black coats, even in summer . . . They are not under government control and receive no grants, but are recognised *de facto* if not *de jure* as exempting boys and their parents from the provisions of the Compulsory Education Law. *Yeshivot*: The central aim . . . is common to all: the study of Torah . . . as it has been studied for hundreds of years, largely individually. You will . . . see 100-200-300 boys or young men, reading their page of Talmud (aloud and all at the same time!)

each to himself or in small groups and swaying to and fro as they read.' [There are instructors to be consulted, and some individual testing] 'but there are no certificates, no diplomas, no degrees, and yet many Yeshivot including those that teach no general subjects – nothing but Talmud and Bible and Musar from morning till night – are full to capacity and with long waiting lists!

These are to some extent, and inevitably, schools of fanaticism and their students sometimes figure in riotous attacks on breaches of orthodoxy – until recently the only examples of student violence to be found in Israel. The author's final comment is apt. 'It is interesting to see that education, where there is faith behind it, can thus hold its own, even "against the stream of time".' That phrase is from a description (which the author quotes on page 8) of the aim of Jewish education, by Rabbi Abraham Isaac Kook, Palestine's first Ashkenazi Chief Rabbi.

A clearly defined stamp has been set on our schools, maintained by devotion and effort *against* the stream of Time, that they shall be centred on the spirit of Israel and its special mission, and that practical training for life shall be sought elsewhere, so that it shall be known that there is a distinction between holy and profane.

Inward-looking religious cells within the framework of a secular society are not peculiar to Israel. But it is hard to think of another example in a Western-style country of such cells dedicated to the aggressive rejection of the whole *ethos* of the surrounding community.

5

Religion

The most evidently paradoxical of all the anomalies on which the Jewish State is founded is so familiar to its people that it is taken for granted. For our purpose it needs to be made explicit.

The Declaration of Independence begins 'In the Land of Israel the Jewish people came into being. In this Land was shaped *their spiritual, religious, and national character*' (italics added). Their spiritual and religious character, as shaped in the Land of Israel, was that of a people committed to the observance of its Law and Teaching in every province and every detail of life. Presumably the Jews of the Diaspora have in part abandoned (or they might say advanced beyond) this total religio-national commitment, since their corporate life as Jews is concerned with religion in its narrower sense and with the affairs of their own denominational community. But the purpose of religious life in Israel, in so far as it is more than self-protective, must ideally be the practice of Judaism in the whole national life of the people. Yet in a later passage the Declaration lays it down that the State 'will guarantee freedom of religion and conscience, of language, education and culture'. This is the language, not of traditional Judaism, but of modern pluralist democracy. Given the inclusion among the citizens of Israel of a majority either hostile to traditional belief or for practical purposes uncommitted to it, there was and is no practical alternative. It is the implications that concern us here.

It may be that, as some believe, when the State was founded the religious authorities thought it only a matter of time before its com-prehensively religious character would be established. In that convic-tion, (in this reading of their position) they took up a defensive posture, content for the time being with the same degree of recognition of religious observance as they had enjoyed under the Mandate. Then, finding the secular ingredient in the population unexpectedly deter-mined to resist further encroachment by religious authority, indeed restive under its current pressures, they became set in their defensive attitude.

Another interpretation, not entirely inconsistent with the first, is that the religious establishment was always permeated by the frame of mind of Jewry in the Diaspora, from which most of the leading figures came. They thought and felt as a minority, content to live as such, with no sense of obligation to reach out towards their non-religious fellow citizens, look for common ground, or strive to find it by grappling with the wider problems confronting a modern State with a religious basis. There is a story, if not true then *ben trovato*, that a certain Chief Rabbi was consulted by a police detective of orthodox leanings, troubled by the many infringements of Sabbath observance which his profession required. What should he do? The advice he got was to find another profession. On a religious Kibbutz, with a corporate ethic powerful enough virtually to rule out crime, this would be a legitimate and practical attitude. In the national community, where being 'like other nations' goes far enough to require the domestic use of force, it is neither. It appears to turn the secular population into a kind of 'Shabbas Goy' – the Arab worker whom the Kibbutzim of the First Aliya employed to do the Sabbath work forbidden to a Jew. For believers, religious authority does go some way to find practical solutions to the problems of observance posed by the conditions of modern life. But its attitude generally is felt, by 'seculars', even at times by religious parties too, to be excessively cautious and resistant. There are sometimes sharp public confrontations, not directly with the religious authorities themselves but with those observant of the Law as they prescribe it. Moreover there is virtually no evidence of concern with urgent problems of personal morality, and none overtly with political issues except the maintenance of extended State boundaries.

There are a few serious attempts to find genuine solutions in the spirit of Jewish teaching to some of the problems of contemporary life. The Religious Zionist party itself is one such. In national politics, though its special concern is chiefly with questions of public observance and the status of Jews, it attempts officially to grapple with the problems of statecraft. Its related activity, the Religious Kibbutz movement, goes deeper: we shall speak of it below. The Religious State Schools, whatever doubts may be entertained about their practical achievements, must be reckoned a genuine attempt to find a synthesis of religious and secular requirements in the teaching of the young. Of the religious University of Bar-Ilan something similar could be said. It was originally opposed both by the orthodox and the secular, and for the same reason: that it was not at all the sort of rabbinical school which they understood and would, respectively, welcome or tolerate. But having first achieved international recognition for its academic standards, it finally won the same accolade from its own reluctant national authorities. The Jewish element in its curricula consists of a 'basic studies' programme in Bible and Talmud, four courses in Jewish Studies, and two of a total of ten courses in Languages and Literatures. There are six courses in the Social Sciences, and eight in Science and Maths. The University incorporates Schools of Education and Social Work, an Institute of Criminology, a recently opened Law Faculty, and an Institute for Local Government.

On the whole, however, religious life in Israel is dominated by a conservative type of clerical authority, flanked on the right (so to speak) by sects even more extreme than itself in their orthodox allegiance, and on the left by a series of dissident individuals, groups or movements, genuine adherents of the faith but reaching out after some more contemporary expression of it. If we start on the extreme right, the place to begin is Neturei Karta, whose very extremism helps to throw light on the entire picture. One of their sympathizers, a British Jew, asks what is for them the crucial question: 'Are we a people whose life is regulated by a supernatural divine order, whose earthly and bodily existence are not dependent on normal political, economic and material successes or failures? A people whose *raison d'être* is wholly bound up with undefinable supernatural ways, with the Torah and its commandments which cannot be fully comprehended by earthly, human reason? Or are we a people which exists, rises and falls, in consequence of the very same factors, which cause all other nations to rise and fall, a nation like any other nation?'[1] The answer that Neturei Karta gives is best shown by the manifesto they issued on 24 May 1967, the day Nasser closed the gulf of Aqabah and made war inevitable.

[margin handwritten note: pure religion anarchists]

> We have no connection with them (the Zionists) or with any of their affairs. We desire no benefit from them or through them, neither deliverance nor protection. Nor do we desire collaboration with them. What have we to do with them? We will stand by this, with the Lord's help, with all our strength. We do not approve of any hatred or hostility and above all of any strife or war in any form against any people, nation, or tongue, since our Holy Torah has not commanded this of us in our Exile, but the

reverse. If, through our many sins, we are apparently joined in the destiny of these rebels, Heaven forbid, all we can do is to pray to the Holy One, Blessed be He, that He may release us from their destiny and deliver us.[2]

This movement has no normal form of organization, no office or postal address, just a membership, and a spiritual leader who lives in Brooklyn, New York, but visits them every year to stiffen their renunciation of the secular state with all its works and organs. One of them wrote publicly, in 1959, 'We cannot avoid using the Zionist post office, but there are those who, as a reminder to themselves, are in the habit of sticking postage stamps upside down and, furthermore, of not mentioning Israel when writing the address.'[3]

Here is what Ben-Gurion wrote of them in a newspaper article in 1954 when he was Prime Minister:

The Guardians of the City are a living remnant, even though embalmed and congealed, of this Judaism, and they have the right to speak in the name of the original and essential Judaism no less than the people of Aguda and Mizrachi [the religious parties]. No-one has the right to use the power of government, even if it is founded on a majority, to suppress a belief that is in the heart.[4]

The difference between Neturei Karta and Aguda is chiefly in the former's total repudiation of secular methods, even under the tremendous pressures of the Nazi persecutions and the Six-Day War. Their religious world-view is otherwise not very different. Aguda, from a similar starting point, was moved by the catastrophe of Nazi persecution to see the divine hand at work in the establishment of the State – a position the religious Zionists, the Mizrachi, had taken up much earlier, in Europe. Here is a statement of the agudist world view, as interpreted in a sympathetic Hebrew newspaper about a decade after Independence.

The world was created for the sake of Israel. It is the duty and merit of Israel to maintain and fulfil the Torah. The place where Israel is destined to live and, therefore, to maintain the Torah, is the Land of Israel. This means that the *raison d'être of the world is the establishment of the regime of the Torah in the Land of Israel* [italics added]. The foundation of this ideal has been laid. There are now Jews living in their homeland and fulfilling the Torah. But completion has not yet been attained, for all Israel does not yet live in its land, not even the majority, and the greater part of the

Promised Land is still in the enemy's hands. Finally, all Israel is not yet fulfilling the Torah . . . It is our duty to complete our mission which must become our innermost concern.[5]

The Religious Zionist party, larger and politically more influential, would share with this statement the ideas that the Jewish people is in Israel by divine right and that its duty and destiny to fulfil the Torah in that Land over-rides other considerations. But it is more aware of the need to take account of the practical requirements of life and government. Moreover, and perhaps a more important difference, its sense of the special and supreme mission of Israel is tempered by the realization that the Almighty is the Lord of all men, and that love and pity are among His attributes and ordinances. It is less given to the expressions of harsh intolerance that mark some other religious groupings. These things are matters of emphasis, and none of the orthodox, nor the Rabbinate itself, will always speak in gentle tones when they feel that essentials are threatened. But there are degrees.

Given that in the cosmic scheme of things Israel is to be thought of as a pilot plant in which the divine design is worked out for the instruction and guidance of the human race, one can understand the intense concern to maintain the integrity of the teaching, the life of the people, and the observance of the one by the other. The unbending religious rigidity illustrated in the 'Who is a Jew?' controversies is defensive, and if – as critics say – the basis of it is fear, the reply might be that to fear disobedience and its consequences is a duty. Modern Jewish history has shown the believer that the road on to which the gates of the ghetto open is commonly a downhill slope. It leads to Christian conversion, or atheism, or at least a half-alienated indifference – all three spelling the end of Israel and the loss of its mission. The rigid orthodoxy we see today was in its historic origins a reaction against the threat posed by enlightenment and emancipation. Today, secularization in Israel and assimilation abroad show how real the possibility of loss of the mission still is.

Nor is this the only thought that makes orthodox believers intransigent. They are sensitive to the perils of disobedience and mindful of past Jewish experience. They suspect the rationalism of the modern Enlightenment: it seems to them naive and superficial. There is a beast in man, ready to leap out and fall upon Jewry, not its only victim but historically its most constant one. The holocaust (the universal Israeli term for the Nazi killing of six million Jews) is a far more vivid reality to those who were scorched by its fierce breath than it can be to others. (Jews are unhappily aware how much less it meant to others.) As a memory it is as recent as the Eichmann trial. Many things about Israel, from outstanding military valour on the one hand to exceptional inflexibility of doctrine on the other, can best be understood in the light of it. It stands as a testimony to the seeming power of evil among men, an awful reminder that in the cosmic drama of the people of Israel there is a villain not to be trifled with. Strict obedience to God's word is required to safeguard, not primarily the human community, but the divine purpose. Its claim on Israel is absolute, be the immediate outcome prosperity or tragedy.

The entire secular approach therefore is seen as – to put it at its mildest – an abandonment of the true path. There can be no distinction between the ethical and the ritual aspects of the code. The Rector of the religious University of Bar-Ilan writes:

> Ritual observance is indeed an integral part of our witness. To understand this may be difficult for a Protestant but there is no alternative to that 'willing suspension of disbelief' which alone can enable the observer from outside to understand Judaism and Jewish history. The very word 'ritual' in English carries a pejorative quality derived from the Protestant tradition. The word in Hebrew is *Mizvot* [religious command] and these have the same moral force whether involving relations between man and man or between man and God. It is the latter part of the code that embodies the so-called ritual commandments, and these are on any proper appraisal as indispensable as the ethical commandments. [6]

This is a statement of doctrine, and not on the face of it a total endorsement of rabbinical policy. There have in fact been for several years past a number of voices speaking from within the ranks of orthodoxy but in partial detachment from the Rabbinate or in open criticism of it. Of detachment, the best and most constructive example is the Religious Kibbutz movement – Kibbutz Dati. Its principal origins were outside Palestine, in Germany, Eastern Europe and in lesser degree the Jewish communities in Western Europe and overseas. By the time of the fight for independence it had set up nine Kibbutzim, mostly on the then borders of Jewish settlement (there are now a dozen). They played a notable and outstandingly valiant part in resisting the invading Arab armies. One of them, Kfar Etzion near Hebron, stood a five months' siege that ended with the killing of most of its male settlers and is vividly remembered as one of the epic stories of that war. The movement was born in the '30s, of disillusion with the life of Jewry, a social religion, as lived in the materialist, competitive societies of the West. That half of the Torah which was concerned not with individual ethics but with the life of a people in their own land had been inoperative since the dispersion. On the foundation of the Kibbutz idea, as already established in Israel, let the Jewish religious tradition be re-established: let it be demonstrated that a socialist collective could be religious too. Thus the basic ideas of this movement are socialism and nationalism, but within the boundaries of Jewish religious tradition. Ten years after Independence it claimed to have made 'an important contribution to contemporary Judaism, in that we have demonstrated the power of halacha to extend its sanctity over everyday life in this modern age.'[7] Once the central significance attached to ritual conformity, as part of the divine ordinance, is understood, it becomes less surprising to find that the examples of their achievement chosen by spokesmen of this movement are apt to be those concerned with solutions to problems of Sabbath or ritual observance. One of them writes, 'A religious community is to be judged not only by the personal conduct of its individual members, but also by its overall aim and the public institutions it succeeds in evolving. . .'. Then, a few lines later, 'A problem which affects us closely, that of milking cows on the Sabbath, will help to clarify this point.'[8]

But in fact this is by no means the whole story. The atmosphere of the religious Kibbutzim, like the good manners of their young people, shows a distinctive influence at work. There is a climate of liberal thought, an openness towards secular learning, and a tone of purposeful mildness. They co-operate closely with the secular Kibbutz groupings over the whole field of practical affairs, and are respected for their combination of profound sincerity with high standards of practical efficiency. Although they would accept the *ex cathedra* pronouncements of the Rabbinate when these clearly involve halachic principles, they resisted (for example) its ban on the military call-up of girls, which they thought no more than an expression of one opinion, against which they were entitled to set their own. Moreover they continue to feel free to turn for guidance on particular problems of applying religious law, not to the Rabbinate but to 'an authority who tends towards leniency', i.e. a rabbi of their own selection. This sort of flexibility, limited as the 'tolerance' is, may suggest the direction of wider change in Israel, if and when altered conditions encourage it.

Meantime the contribution they make to the life of the State is unique and may prove to have great significance. They consciously and loyally apply the teachings of Judaism both ethical and ritual over a wider province of life than any other institution in Israel known to the author. They bear the fullest witness to the practical meaning of Judaism as a social religion. They make their living chiefly by agriculture but there seems no reason why they should not extend their economic range without departing from their principles. But they are not a political community in the full sense. Though actively associated with one party (Mizrachi) and individually influential within it, they are a small minority group and so cannot as such face the supreme test of a national religion – that of direct responsibility for political decision. How far their influence will extend depends partly on their own flexibility, partly on that of institutional religion.

Another possible line of development is of an entirely different kind: religious disestablishment. This naturally has many advocates among the secular, but some also on the religious side. There may be more of these than can be traced and are certainly more than can be quoted; some thinkers of irreproachable orthodoxy are convinced that rabbinical authority of any kind is a phase that has had its day. As the Temple gave place to the synagogue, the scribes to the sages, and the rabbi as judge-legislator to the rabbi as pastoral teacher, all without prejudice to the essential continuity, so another kind of leadership may emerge and in due time take over. Short of such daring private speculation, there is already open and radical criticism of the present connection between religion and the State. One of its spokesmen since the early days of the State has been Pinhas Rosenblüt, head of religious education in Mikve Israel, the famous agricultural training institution. He has campaigned for a more active attempt on the part of rabbinical authority to reach out to the community, establish a dialogue, explain the significance of religion, and formulate a programme – 'a common modicum of *mitzvot* as a foundation for the community's life'. This he said would be a more positive approach than mere complaints about desecration. The religious community can achieve a great deal by creating new social forms in which to meet fellow citizens of various opinions. Community projects such as joint social groups, parents' committees and study groups, could do much to exchange opinions and hammer out differences. In his view the religious authorities have neither set out to include the social life and problems of Israel within a religious framework, as the traditional character of Judaism might have indicated, nor spoken distinctive words about the great moral and social questions facing society, from the confrontation with the Arabs to the changed situation of women. The association of 'Church' and State in Dr Rosenblüt's opinion gave the former the worst of both worlds – it left the 'secular' alienated and out of reach, without fostering any sense of responsibility for positive action by the religious. The association should be ended.

There has also been more recently an effort in the same direction with some organization behind it. The entire *status quo*, the involvement of the religious establishment with the State, has been persistently criticized by Professor Urbach of the Hebrew University, an orthodox Jew who in 1966 founded a 'movement for Judaism of the Torah'. Two basic Resolutions passed at its Conference during Passover 1968 ran:

(a) Every citizen or resident in Israel is entitled to full freedom in matters of faith, religion and observance, and has the right, together with his fellows, to be organised in a community for the performance of matters of faith and observance.

(b) Every organised public activity, including election of recognised Doctors of Law and Rabbinical Courts, shall be entrusted exclusively to the communities which shall be freely organised for this purpose by free election of the residents in every locality under State Law.

Urbach has conducted an active campaign of meetings aimed at separating religion entirely from politics, so setting it free to seek fuller contact and communication with the life of the community, and to relate the halacha more significantly to contemporary life. He calls for dynamic change. He has written, 'Is this generation ready to be not just bnai halacha – the children of the halacha, but bonai halacha – the builders of the halacha in the religious sense of the word? In the answer to this question lies the future of the Jewish religion.'

It is relevant also to recall some words written in 1964 by a writer associated with the religious Kibbutz movement:

The entire policy of the religious parties is doomed to failure so long as it is not supplemented by a serious effort on the non-political level to bring the non-religious to a serious confrontation with the religious issue on the level of faith and personal commitment. The rabbinic leadership is unable to do this. Their policy of cultural retrenchment renders them incapable of entering into genuine communication with the non-religious in this respect.[9]

There is no intention to suggest that these views are widely representative or have yet had much practical impact. They are outlined here for a different reason – in fact for three. They show that it has been possible for bold spirits, holding positions of unquestionable orthodoxy, to utter from their own point of view the same criticisms of the religious establishment as can be heard from the secular side, and to do it just as incisively. Secondly, to set out these views is enough to show the gap between such an approach and the attitude to their duties that the Rabbinate and the religious parties have in fact taken, and their imperviousness thus far to any suggestion of a positive or crusading attitude to the situation that confronts them. Thirdly, there may here be a hint of the sort of ideas that might gain currency if ever the authorities, without compromising their halachic loyalties in principle, felt able to relax their defensive posture and adopt a more out-going policy towards the majority of the community.

There are outposts in Israel of the two great non-orthodox movements in the United States, Conservative and Reform Judaism (in British terms 'reform' and 'liberal' respectively). The former, which one might call a sort of liberal orthodoxy, numbers among its American membership some eminent theologians, and sponsors Jewish educational institutions of high standing. In Israel its impact is most felt in the educational field. Reform Judaism established its first synagogue in Jerusalem in 1958 and in the next eight years added six others in as many more towns. It has had a school in Haifa since 1939 and a college and Archaeological School in Jerusalem since 1963. But despite a thorough-going change of heart in recent decades its reputation among Israelis is still slightly shadowed by the anti-Zionist phases of its earlier history. Though these were abandoned long ago they are sometimes publicly recalled in the Israeli press. Perhaps slightly for this reason, but more because its religious activities have not been widely accepted as relevant to Israeli life and problems, its progress there has evidently been a disappointment to its Israeli pioneers and American sponsors. In a community partly founded upon the idea that the identity of religion and nationalism calls for practical expression in a State, there are inevitably some obstacles to acceptance of the claims of Jewish denominations which were born of the opposite assumption, however impeccable their Zionist loyalties may be. This question is involved with the wider one of the relations between Israel and the Diaspora.

There is a group of about fifty people in Jerusalem, started in 1962, which disavows the title of 'movement' and calls itself 'Seekers of the Way'. It holds Sabbath services in very informal style, with a period for questions from the congregation, and calls occasional conferences. Its main significance is perhaps in the idea for which it stands – that the methods of outward expression of religious life in Judaism, the ceremonial rules and the liturgies, have always been historically conditioned, and are therefore bound to go on responding flexibly to the needs of the day and to the character of the environment. While its leaders would disclaim any formal link with the 'Reconstructionist' movement in the United States, there are recognizable ideas in common.

That same year, 1962, saw another development outwardly quite different in kind, but equally a sign of radical discontent with the state of religious life in Israel, on the part of people who took religion seriously. There was started in Tel Aviv a magazine, hopefully described as bi-monthly, to be devoted to religious thought. It was called *Prozdor* – one might say entrance hall, or porch. In its introductory editorial it declared:

This periodical 'Prozdor' will be devoted to religious thought. Strange as it may seem to a nation which gave to half of humanity its religious life, it is nevertheless true that in our modern Hebrew literature there isn't yet, or there is no longer, room for the religious thought. . . . The manner in which our official religion bears itself in public is not likely to enhance its prestige. Our youth is growing up without knowing at all what religion is. Our wide public discussions of religion deal mainly with practical matters, like problems of matrimony, *halitza*, or mixed bathing of men and women in a swimming pool. . . . But religious thought as such has no place with us. . . . In problems of theology and religion, the level of our discussions and deliberations is absolutely childish. Whilst our brethren overseas have organs of expression devoted to problems of religious thought, we have in our country no instrumentality for deliberations on these questions.

For over five years, until its demise in October 1967, *Prozdor* published articles, often from distinguished pens, on metaphysics and theology, on the perennial secular-religious issue in Israel, on education, and general cultural subjects. Occasionally there were specific suggestions for restoring Jewish life and values. All these are interesting for the attitudes they suggest. Some have achieved a limited realization in recent years. One writer would set up exemplary Jewish institutions –

synagogues to replace what he saw as the existing ugly dreary ones, schools to replace the poor-quality Religious State schools and the narrow, out-dated Talmud Torah and Yeshivot. Another would form small groups to create a new Jewish way of life – groups in Kibbutzim, Moshavim, the towns. Their basic programme would be to build up a sense of communal purpose and responsibility: to live a life of simplicity and modesty; to bring up to date traditional forms of prayer; to develop contemporary ritual forms that would reflect the life of the people. Yet a third proposal echoed this same idea – 'The formulation of a religious way of life can only come about through the activities of small groups of individual searchers who can serve as an example for others.'

Immediately after the war, in its last gallant double issue, the editors explained the reasons for its failure – 'a compound of financial difficulties and lack of a sufficient number of active Israeli contributors on subjects to which *Prozdor* was devoted.' The first is a common enough reason for the failure of highbrow publishing ventures: the second, shortage of writers, would be unusual in any country with respectable standards of culture and is doubly and trebly so in 'the nation which gave to half of humanity its religious life'. Thus in the middle half of the '60s Israel's intellectual élite had not enough appetite for religious discussion on its own wave-length to sustain either as writers or readers a journal devoted to it. Perhaps the fundamental challenge was not yet apparent.

The Six-Day War left nothing and no one unchanged – 'The shortest war in our history, casting the longest shadow', said one Kibbutz philosopher. Its immediate effects were naturally to concentrate all minds on the urgent problems facing the State and to remind them of the over-riding need for national unity. The tremendous emotional experience of sudden acute peril, weeks of suspense, and almost instant victory left the orthodox religious strengthened in their convictions and confirmed in their attitudes. To adopt Aneurin Bevan's *mot*, they had no need to look in the crystal: they could read the books.

Among most of the ultra-orthodox and in the rabbinical schools and colleges there arose a fresh impulse of political messianism, an intensified sense of destiny being fulfilled, a seeming awareness that a late chapter in Israel's story was beginning to unfold. Here, visible again, was the miraculous thread of promise and fulfilment that had run in one strand from the deliverance of Isaac, through the Exodus, through three

thousand years of preservation, to the two miracles of their own day:
first the transformation in three years of a hell of degradation in the
Nazi camps into the free citizenship of a sovereign state, and now –
now this exalting, humbling deliverance in six days from the arrogant
menaces of another Pharaoh, whose heart the Lord had again hardened
to his undoing. In the rabbinical schools, a generation of their pupils
is being thus indoctrinated. There grew up, too, a Land of Israel
Movement, enjoying notable religious support, dedicated to the
retention of all the occupied territory, maintaining indeed that no
secular government had the right to hand it back. One of its active
supporters is the Rector of Bar-Ilan, Dr Fisch, who speaks of it as
'possibly the first political movement in modern Jewish history in which
differences between Right and Left, secular and religious, have faded
away through the equalising force of a newfound Jewish identity' and
describes it as 'pervaded by an over-arching sense of historical challenge
and responsibility which with hardly any exaggeration could be called
religious'.[10] More than a year later Dr Fisch wrote,[11]

It is my position (and I am sure that this is also the position of the
majority) that there is only one nation to whom the land belongs
in trust and by covenant, and that is the Jewish people. No
temporary demographic changes can alter this basic fact which is
one of the principles of our faith. Just as one wife does not have
two husbands so one land does not have two sovereign nations
in possession of it. You will understand that the covenant analogy
is what links these two terms together, but then even the covenant
of marriage depends for its maintenance upon a minimum of faith
on the part of those entering into it.

The war thus cast an even more intense light upon what had always
been part of the essence of the religio-national tradition of Judaism –
the link with the Land. Let us dwell on it for a moment. At this point
the orthodoxies of Judaism and of secular Zionism meet. Such a
geographical transfer as has been accepted by another people whose
nationalism is passionate and obdurate, the Poles, would be unthinkable to the Israeli Jew. If we find ourselves at this point on the edge of
mysticism, the myth, and the constantly repeated biblical promises in
which it is rooted, have some history to sustain them. There have been
no other instances in which the world has been compelled to reverse
totally in twenty years an ethnic 'image' which it had entertained and
acted on for nearly two thousand. It is strange, too, that the populous

and fertile land of Bible times should have been depopulated and beggarly for most of two millennia, and then within a few years have begun again to flow with milk and honey. It is an odd quirk that in the three thousand years and more of its known political history the only times Palestine has been more than a cockpit for the wars of great empires, or a minor province of some one of them, have been when it was a State under Jewish sovereignty. A Jew hardly needs to be a mystic to see some correspondence between the fates of his people and of their land, or to think that the two belong together. One of Israel's most brilliant teachers has written: 'If we want to borrow from the vocabulary of Christian theology we might say that Jewish existence is an incarnational existence. . . . To invite the Jews to live as Jews and to be faithful to "Judaism" without fulfilling their existence in . . . the hypostatic union of people and land is sheer hypocrisy.'[12]

By no means all devotees of the mystique of the land would infer from this a present claim to the whole of it. But many do and this includes many orthodox Jews. It certainly, and rather surprisingly, includes a substantial part of the Religious Kibbutz Movement, whose Zionism has proved itself in war but whose spirit gives no obvious impression of militancy. Yet its post-war attempt to give to Judaism a more contemporary reference included one unexpected element. It brought out in 1968 a book of prayers and poems including a prayer for recital on Independence Day, the anniversary of the State, not then recognized by the Rabbinate as a religious holiday. This ran, 'Extend the boundaries of our Land, just as Thou has promised our forefathers, from the river Euphrates to the river of Egypt. Build your holy city, Jerusalem, capital of Israel; and there may your temple be established as in the days of Solomon.'[13] Solomon's site is regarded by some of the orthodox as a holy place; it is now occupied by the two great Moslem shrines, the Dome of the Rock and the Mosque of Aqsa. A representative member of the Religious Kibbutz Movement, asked to throw further light on this prayer, wrote,[14] 'When a Jew prays he doesn't pray only for his own sake or for the sake of his people, he prays also for the whole world. Thus the prayers have a universal significance. . . .' Then he quotes from a prayer recited three times daily, ending with the words of Zachariah, 'And the Lord shall be King over all the earth: in that day shall there be one Lord, and his name one'. He continues, 'When we pray to extend the Land and establish the Temple we think of those great days ahead of us'. A distinction can of course be drawn between an acceptance of the vision of Zachariah and hawkish politics.

The Religious Kibbutzim do not as such support the Land of Israel Movement, though some of their membership do. They are moved by the fact that the occupation, unwilled and unsought by Israel, yet happened. Not only they but other religious Jews have felt since the Six-Day War that this outcome of a fight with Jordan which they tried hard to avoid is evidence of the divine hand at work, and that they should accept it, as they had accepted peaceably the restricted boundaries within which they formerly lived. One of them said to the author that to give up the 'territories' now would be as serious a breach of Covenant as to break a consummated marriage, and that the internal effects on the people of Israel would be dangerously frustrating and disruptive.

On the other hand, very different ideas about the War have been expressed by a variety of religious intellectuals, devout men deeply concerned for the reality of the Jewish faith though by no means conformists to the policies of the Establishment. Many of them write for and help to conduct the journal *Petahim*, founded partly as successor to *Prozdor*, soon after the Six-Day War. As is natural after that experience, its focus of interest is nearer to concrete, practical issues than was its more theologically disposed predecessor. Some of its contributors have maintained firmly that the War had no special religious significance, that no war could have, and that it was no more 'miraculous' than any other terrestrial event. Others, the majority, saw in it a profound religious significance, not as in itself a fulfilment of the divine will but as a national opportunity, a spiritual challenge which given a valid response could open a way towards fulfilment of the mission of the people of Israel. The desired response was variously described as an act of reflection, of will, of decision – a rising to the height of moral and spiritual opportunity through prayer and study; something that would lead to a fuller realization in the community of the true values of Jewish ethical teaching. There is further reference to *Petahim* in the next chapter.

6

Non-Religion?

The wits in Israel will tell you that the population is made up of those who have come to be Jews in safety and those who have come to be non-Jews in comfort. Over against the religious establishment, its critics from within, its fringe dissidents and intellectuals, is an equal number either indifferent to religion or positively hostile to it. What are the numbers? This is a suitable point at which to introduce the numerical picture of divided religious opinion, as the techniques of sociological investigation have revealed it over the past few years. It seems that in that period about one in ten of the Jewish population claim to adhere strictly to traditional practice, and as many again to do so fairly strictly – amounting to one in five who can be called observant. At the other end of the scale about 30 per cent say they are completely non-observant. In the middle are about half the population who say they keep the tradition 'to a certain extent'. These categories are vague, especially the last: but what is known about synagogue attendance confirms and refines the figures given. Thus about one in five go to synagogue either every day (6 per cent) or just about every Sabbath and holiday. One in five never go: one in four only once (on the Day of Atonement) and the rest, roughly a third, 'several times a year'. By relating the two sets of detailed figures, it is possible to calculate that of the half or so who are 'to a certain extent' observant some 15 per cent (that is, nearly a third of the half) confine their synagogue attendance to one annual visit. It seems safe to say that many of this group attend out of habit, respect for tradition, or regard for their families, rather than for any genuine religious purpose. The same must be true of the more infrequent of those who attend 'several times a year'. In short, the community is made up of a fifth who are fully observant, something between 40 per cent and 50 per cent who are completely 'secular' or nearly so, and the rest – say a third – who are in varying degrees partially observant. It is known that Israelis of

72

oriental or African birth or descent are at the outset much more 'religious' than the average, and that their beliefs tend to assimilate to those of the culturally dominant majority – those of Western descent. This is one reason for expecting a further shift away from observance to secular habits as time goes on. Another reason is a shift in that direction already observable – the results of inquiries made at intervals. Yet another is the fact that school children reveal themselves less tied to traditional ways than their parents, or teachers. Finally, and most strikingly, a survey among leaders of opinion in a wide range of occupations shows them, apart from the 'hard core' of the orthodox, markedly more 'secular' than the general population. An inquiry made in 1969 showed nearly half the total completely non-observant and over a third describing themselves as 'a little' observant. Similarly, over 40 per cent of this group never went to synagogue and another one in seven only on the Day of Atonement.

Two more details of some significance. Asked how much influence the Jewish religion had on their own sense of themselves as Jews, about 30 per cent indicated that it had a good deal, another 30 per cent that it had little or none (surely a surprising figure) and the other 40 per cent or so that it had 'some'. The Asians and Africans included in the sample were a good deal more attached to the religious aspect of their Jewish identity – the proportion who gave religion little or no share in it was only about half that of the rest. It follows that among the latter, the 'trend-setting' majority, the fraction who ascribed to religion little or no share in their sense of themselves as Jews must have been well over a third.

What is it that underlies and explains the indifference or hostility of the large middle section of opinion? It was to be expected in a community partly drawn from the half-secularized Jewish communities of the West and largely shaped by the secular religion of Zionism. It was this latter, especially in its most influential and formative expressions on the Kibbutzim, but also in the towns, that gave to the more distinctive secular attitudes in Israel their special character and their significance for the future.

The pioneer generation were revolutionaries, with a fighting creed of socialist idealism, a religion of non-religion. They worked their way to possession of a Land they had in the most literal and physical of senses made their own and then fought to keep; their struggle brought them also the great bonus of political freedom. But when this newly independent community began to reproduce itself, the generation of seculars born during the years around the foundation of the State showed some characteristics that had not been foreseen, though perhaps they might have been. The bulk of the Sabras (the Israel-born) were innocent not only of any cosmic vision but of any awareness of the world around them. A magazine of the mid-'50s carried a cartoon based on a map of the world that had actually been drawn by a schoolchild in Afula; it showed two hemispheres, one filled with the recognizable outlines of Israel, the other with a vague round object labelled 'other lands'. But there was worse than ignorance: there was alienation.

The tough, practical, down-to-earth type bred by the life of the new nation was out of tune with the crusading ideology of the genera-tion before it. The land, to their parents a vision brought to earth, had become the unquestioned setting for their daily occupations. Their homes, won brick by brick, they took for granted. Their freedom they valued no more than the air they breathed – it was in the nature of things. The Zionist ideal had been achieved. Why go on about it, as their elders were apt to go on, not only in public meeting halls but in their own living-rooms? 'Zionizing' became a term of derision – a little like 'King and Country' to some of the young in the Britain of the '30s. This was all the more so since lofty idealism was by no means always realized in the life they saw around them, especially on those Kibbutzim where the high moral purposes of communal life had declined into the joint pursuit of materialist objectives. In Mexico, the name of the governing party is the Institutional Revolutionary Party: Israel's secular revolution had, for its young generation, become institutionalized. When a revolution is institutionalized, it is blighted – that is unless it retains an inner vitality strong enough to maintain growth and keep its outward forms flexible. For the Sabras, what force could that be?

Religious teaching there was none for them: the cultural traditions of Judaism had no inner meaning: the days of ceremony might be anything from a pagan shell to a deliberate parody. The spiritual values of the exile – the values of suffering, the courage that endures and does not yield – were not only rejected, they were despised. As long ago as 1930 men who could penetrate beneath the surface of the new life had seen this coming. In a story called 'The Sermon', by a well known Israeli writer, Hayim Hazaz, a young Russian immigrant is made to say: 'I oppose Jewish history. We do not have a history at all because we did not make our history; it was the doing of the Goyim. . . . It bores me to death. . . . I know there is heroism in the fact that we could withstand all this harassment, but I don't like such heroism.' As for Jewish culture, 'It is a very funny culture: . . . it is a world of darkness, of negativeness. Their sorrow became an ideal, not their happiness. Their pain became more understandable than their happiness; destruction more than construction; slavery more than redemption; the dream more than reality; and hope for an undetermined future more than common sense. It is a psychology of night.' These passages were quoted in 1969 in an address by Mr Mordechai Bar-On, one of the best known of the younger generation, who could himself confirm how true they remained to the feelings of youth in the years after the story was written. They are quoted here at length because they are authentic notes that the visitor can still hear echoed in the talk of the young: the young who have felt and proved their own strength.

They felt cut off not only from their own past, but from their fellow-Jews abroad too. What was this wonderful Zionism that could not bring Jews to Israel unless they were driven there – and not always then if they had another country to go to, like the Jews evicted from Algeria who went to France? Who were these disinherited brethren in America and Europe who were unmoved by the wide open gates of the Promised Land? Did they *like* their exile? Was there something to be said for disinheritance?

Young Israelis of this type did not for the most part disavow their Jewishness: they ignored it. They thought of themselves as Israelis: that was something they felt, understood, and could take some pride in. For the rest – a shrug. Hear again the abrasive voice of ultra-orthodoxy: 'Has not the fulfilment of the greatest Zionist aspiration resulted in a crop of infidels with which no other country outside Communist Russia can compare?'[1] This was a state of mind not general, but not uncommon among children of parents with no positive religious commitment. Young people in whose background religion, at least in its outward forms, played some mild part, either gave to their titular faith a lukewarm acknowledgment, or drifted away from it. Those with a positive religious upbringing for the most part followed the traditional ways. But they were the minority.

The minority was increasing, but that was for a special, perhaps temporary reason. It was swollen by the traditionally faithful Jews who poured in, with their children, in the ten or fifteen years after the war: Jews from Tunis, Morocco, Egypt, Iraq, the Yemen. They had brought their beliefs and folkways with them, and by the mid-'60s it was still too early to be quite sure how the secular climate of a modern society would work upon them. But the signs did not suggest they would long resist its permeation. In any event they exerted no such influence as their numbers might have warranted on the spiritual life of the community.

To the young Sabras, products of secular Zionism, the shock of the Six-Day War came as a personal, painful challenge. By what right were they there? Since their claim was not based on religious faith, what did it amount to? Those who had seen the horror of war at first hand, the piled-up corpses of their pitiable enemies, the charred or mutilated bodies of their friends, felt in such questions an even sharper edge.

The great majority, less reflective, more conventional, did not stop long with such doubts. But some did – on the Kibbutzim, among students, among professional thinkers. Their doubts and searches opened or reopened the question of their relation to the Jewish tradition, of who and what they were. Their thoughts and questionings are very well documented. This must put the inquirer on his guard against giving too much weight to such evidence merely because it is available. The question is how representative it is. The author's own conclusion is that it may well prove significant. The Kibbutz conversations about the War, which began within a few weeks of its end, were confined to a few score people: but these few were widely spread, and the records of what they said to one another, printed in October 1967 in the book *Siach Lochamim*,[2] aroused an interest as widespread and spontaneous as official war books like *The Battle of Britain* and *Target for Tonight* did in besieged Britain in the early '40s. (Its sale of 70,000 copies in Israel is equivalent to about a million and a half copies in Britain.) The memories and musings of mere specialized minorities do not evoke such responses.

Much of the content of this first record matches the writings of the British soldier-poets of the two world wars. It was to be expected of any sensitive, educated young soldiers suddenly thrust into the hell of organized slaughter with modern weapons. The Israelis' awareness of and compassion for their enemy as a fellow human being was perhaps keener. Some had lived and worked alongside Arabs, others felt the ingrained Jewish awareness of what it is to endure and sacrifice – 'for sufferance is the badge of all our tribe.' They were also perhaps conscious, a little more than average, of the moral issues raised by war, for as Kibbutzniks they had had the values of communal living drilled into them. Artificial boundaries between groups of human beings were, for some of them, not obviously final. Many of course felt their identity with the Jewish past, as they captured places with Biblical names. Some felt they were writing a new Biblical chapter, or that Gideon was still their captain. To some – not all – this historic link was itself enough to justify their re-occupation: the land was theirs. To others the sense of Jewish identity was sharpened in another way. There were young soldiers who had felt no link with Jews abroad: the sudden realization of the menace that overhung them made them feel closer than they had ever done to the ghetto Jew of the past, and also, in a relation of mutual dependence, to the Jew in the Diaspora today. Some indeed felt protective towards him: there must be no more holocausts – the army of Israel would be there to fight. The influence of the religious was at times evident: there was one unforgettable episode of a commanding officer who came from a religious Kibbutz bandying Bible texts with his men, finally silencing the doubters out of a medieval commentary, and so completing a successful effort to persuade them to stop looting. The soldier who afterwards told of this said, 'I stood in a corner and I thought to myself, "What a peculiar army this is, standing there and listening to all this stuff." But there really was something in it.' Some were uneasy about their role as conquerors, and questioned the rights it conferred. There were arguments between the uncomplicated men who accepted without question the 'normal' action of self-defence, and the more reflective, occasionally rather self-righteous ones who saw a special Jewish character and role in the army's performance.

Finally there were those to whom the entire experience of war was intolerable except as preliminary to self-examination and self-change. More conversations on the Kibbutzim were organized, and the results published.[3] Although the resumption led to some rather forced, self-conscious and often inconclusive talking, it had one additional interest. Preoccupation with the fresh and highly emotional experience of war had gone. Even in *Soldiers' Talk* there had been some concern for the underlying questions it had raised about the position of Jews in Israel, what their Jewishness meant, what obligations it imposed, what message the 'Tradition' carried. This time there was much more.

This second book strikes many as rambling and inconclusive. There are many more questions than answers. Indeed it amounts as a whole to one large, confused question-mark. But the questioning is about something – the meaning of Jewish identity – and its very persistence, from various angles, amounts to a sort of commitment. No doubt religious Jews would relate the confusion and inconclusive-ness to the implicit (occasionally explicit) rejection of faith in the normal sense, and to the obvious ignorance most of the young people show of the content of the religious tradition. But the overall impression left is that things were not going to be allowed to rest at that: the book is a staging post on a road that is intended to lead somewhere. The talks had possibly taken place in the spring of 1969. The author was in Israel at that time and again a year later: in 1970 he heard on all hands and saw for himself that the pursuit of the questions raised in these talks had continued, widened and intensified. Although they were based on the Kibbutzim they echoed and re-echoed outside. Students in the towns show their own interest unmistakably, by the readiness of quite large numbers to attend extra-curricular classes and seminars on relevant subjects. A magazine, *Shdemot* ('Fields'), edited by a group of Kibbutzniks that includes some of the moving spirits behind *Soldiers' Talk*, is published in Tel Aviv on behalf of all three secular groups of Kibbutzim: it deals with religious, political, institutional and cultural themes of interest to young people and is bought and read well beyond the limits of Kibbutz membership.

As we shall see, among these secular young people's responses to the War are various attempts to make contact with the ideas and practices of Judaism: so it is relevant to mention here the group meetings for the study of Jewish subjects which forty or fifty young Kibbutz members attend half a dozen times a year. Here is a descriptive note by one of them:

We soon found that we had in common a *hunger*, accumulated over the years and accentuated after the War, to return to ourselves, to learn the questions and meanings which had occupied our forefathers, whose 'fault' it is that we are what we are and not otherwise. From meeting to meeting we moved 'inwards' and 'backwards', to the depth of the problems of Judaism. From the moderns: Gordon and Rav Kook, and Buber and Borochov, we went back to the sources: the Land and the Promise, Israel as a Chosen People, communal sharing, Sanctification of the Name, Destruction and Redemption. Gradually these concepts appeared to us no longer strange but, on the contrary, convincing by their inner truth, and answering as if by an echo, as if rising from the depths of the soul, to our questions and aspirations.

This is not more than a beginning. There should be no pressure to demand 'faith', or 'practical aims'. Are we only a negligible minority in a sea of apathy, or the advance-guard of an army? It

is too soon to tell. What is certain is that we have travelled a
great distance from where we set out at the beginning of the year.

This extract is quoted from the intellectual magazine *Petahim* ('Gates')
founded in November 1967, to which we have referred.

It can still be maintained that none of this makes much impact on the
large majority of Israelis, even of Kibbutzniks, who are either untouched
by or uncommitted to Judaism in any religious sense. Let the 'natural
man' speak for himself. Here are two passages from *Talks Among Young
People*:

In my opinion, this book [*Soldiers' Talk*] is tendentious. . . . The
people who were selected to take part in it were chosen before-
hand, according to their opinions. The result was . . . unbalanced
. . . and this in its turn led to a negative attitude to the book
among many youngsters who think differently about the war.
Four days ago the funeral of a friend of mine, a pilot who was
killed, took place. . . . The Military Rabbis came and recited all
their psalms, and their Kadishim. This made me and the others
who were there very angry. That pilot, like all of us who joins
the army, do so to protect themselves, their homes and their
country, and nothing else. . . . But the Rabbis repeated again and
again that he died entirely for the sake of God, that supreme God
and supreme power for whose sake we live. This makes me
think . . . that we have reached the point where Jewry is finished,
having completed its role. We have now the State of Israel. Up
till now we were Jews. Now we are Israelis. We defend our
country as Israelis. I do not understand the aspiration of returning
to tradition. I am astonished at the excitement that seized those
who freed the Western Wall. I cannot understand it . . .

For a balanced picture this point of view is an essential component.
It may even be more widely representative than the soul-searchings of
others. Whether it is of greater significance for the future is the very
question mark that hangs over Israel and so over this book. But it
should be remembered that any religious or cultural revival, in any
country, would present a similar picture in its earlier stages. As Emer-
son said, every change begins as a personal opinion. Great trends must
start small; this one is growing; and in any event the rule of the Spirit
is not by majority.

Nor are these stirrings by any means confined to the Kibbutzim.

Dr J. J. Cohen, head of Hillel House, the club for students in the Hebrew University, has written: 'There are literally hundreds of little groups in Kibbutzim, moshavim, towns and cities, in which spiritually concerned men and women have been searching for a way of life which will be the next stage in Jewish religious development.' The present author attended a meeting of one such group recently formed in a Moshav not far from Tel Aviv. Fifteen or twenty people, mostly of parental age, few of them positively religious, had invited an experienced orthodox scholar to conduct a course of lecture seminars on the basic ideas of the Jewish faith. One of his injunctions to them was that 'the biggest mitzva is to build up Judaism in this village'. The group meets in supplement to Sabbath services, in a 'synagogue and community centre' building given by a benefactor. The older attendants at the normal synagogue services grow fewer, the children stay away, the parents want 'something for their children'. Not feeling ready to attend the nearest Reform synagogue they set about informing themselves 'what Judaism is all about'. The approach is experimental – will the courses give them the values they seek to understand, and lead them to the point where they can benefit from services? Perhaps in a year or two (they say) they may have their own form of Sabbath eve service.

Let us now get away from descriptive generalizations, and devote a few pages to people's own accounts of their reflections and searches. Some of these are from the author's notes of conversations, some from the book *Bein Zeirim*, one is a discussion reported in the magazine *Petahim*. We will begin with summary records of four talks in March 1969 on secular Kibbutzim from near the Gaza Strip to Upper Galilee. The names are disguised.

Sam: A small group of us, about a dozen, are holding services now. It started when some of the young people began visiting Habad (the Hasidic village near Jerusalem). Those people's joy and liveliness, and their fervour which is infectious, made quite an appeal. We have no synagogue and have to borrow the scrolls of the law from another kibbutz. We get big attendances at the big festivals, but there's no carryover in between. When I go to our little service, Rachel takes the children to the pool. We aren't orthodox and use the Reform prayer-book because it's simpler. The trouble is we don't know enough about the Books and haven't a teacher or leader. When Shlomo has finished his final religious exams in town next year he may be able to start a study

group. We want some intellectual content – we want to understand what underlies it all. It's plain enough that the old traditions
don't fit any more, and they take up too much time. The young
people aren't interested in the Rabbinate or its ideas – whatever
they are. Given enough study of the books, some of us on the
kibbutzim may be able to create our own tradition – something
that'll have meaning for our children, and theirs.

Amnon: When the older people came originally they were in
revolt against injustice, but these old issues are dead, and we
younger ones have to find our own way to faith. Israel is becoming
less ideological and more pragmatic. We aren't interested in the
politics of religion, but we want to come to contemporary terms
with the Jewish code. On this kibbutz the Passover Hagadah
[initial service] used to be a kind of secular charade but now we're
nearly back to the traditional form: it's because the service is about
deliverance and that's contemporary enough. [Author's note:
this seems to be true of Passover on a large number of secular
settlements.]

Shaul: My grandfather worked all his life to lay the foundations
here and found his fulfilment in it. Now the nation-state is
established, and I feel a lack. I want a purpose. I can't believe in
God, but I want a goal that's beyond realisation in purely human
terms. I think others here do too, though not the majority.

Yitzhak: We must keep our sense of mission and accept the tasks
laid on us as a chosen people. We have to find our religious
fulfilment through social or communal life. This is a secular
kibbutz – yes, but we have a kind of organisation that is morally
advanced: no police, no courts, we keep order without. The
kibbutzim in Israel do have a practical impact: you can see it in
the Army, and in the administration of the occupied territories,
where about 250 Israelis look after a million Arabs. We have a big
problem of change and adjustment here. The Jews always have
had it. Ritual itself was always changing, in the days when it was
being formed, and it will change again. The secular kibbutzim are
the likeliest places for it to happen, because they're freer. What
we need is Time, and Patience.

Next, a note of a talk a year later on a secular Kibbutz in the north.

G. had been completely secular. It was the Eichmann trial which
roused him to the Jewish situation in the world and added a

dimension to his life. 'I became not just an Israeli but a Jew. My purpose now is to identify more with the Jewish heritage.' He is studying Jewish philosophy at Tel Aviv. Will it take him beyond study or teaching, through the strata of culture, to the heart of the tradition? He doesn't know. 'What troubles me in Israel is not physical security – I don't doubt it.' He is concerned about all those spiritually defenceless youngsters. 'We send our boys to the Canal, fully trained, well equipped, but spiritually stripped.' He never imagined the need to face so long and stern a spiritual test as now clearly confronts them. They need spiritual strength, and where can they turn but to Judaism? 'It gave us strength for two thousand years, and what did that was not the military successes but the power of resistance shown under persecution. Look at the Jews in Russia, cut off and brow-beaten but still there.' He quoted the brave parachute commander in *Soldiers' Talk*[4] who said he drew more strength from the thought of the Jews in exile than from the story of the Maccabees. So this again comes back to the need to explore and understand the tradition. But when he thinks of his *national* spiritual objective he feels frustration. The militancy and rigidity of the orthodox are a stumbling block in the path of young seekers, and of his own group in its efforts to find a way forward.

In his reaching out for some spiritual armour he realises the need to keep standards of national conduct pure. 'Jewish nationalism is different because Judaism is a religion, as well as a country and a national group. Our truth is the Jewish truth and we have to try to go deeper to understand it. We have a mission to others because there may be a great need for this truth. We have to achieve spiritual centres everywhere and also keep our base secure. But I'm a bit frightened when I realise that the Arabs have rights too, almost as strong as ours.'

Next, a shortened extract from *Bein Zeirim*:

I think that in the present situation there is no choice but a serious return to tradition. I don't think we can return to religion, to the style of Neturei Karta, nor is that desirable. But I think that the calculated cut-off that came from some notion about creating an original culture, a workers' culture, or something – this calculated cut-off has not succeeded and has not justified itself. The stage we are at now is some sort of return in the direction of Jewish knowledge, in the direction of the Jewish People and our link to the Jewish People . . .

It seems that the question of nationalism is one that occupies the whole world – and we can't just cut ourselves off from the Jewish People, either. It seems that when a person seeks his personal identity, he needs some link with a nation, with something defined. It is very hard for the overwhelming majority of mankind to find their identity as Universal People . . .

Maybe it's our tragedy that if we were able to assimilate, and if we could say: Enough of this people that has existed 3,000 years; we are the generation that is going to put an end to it – fine, we'll end this chain of suffering, we'll assimilate with the Arabs, or with the other nations of the world, and finish. . . . Why do we need all these wars and struggles? But the fact is that we can't do that, and it doesn't depend entirely on our own reason; our emotions and feelings are involved . . . we cannot under any circumstances assimilate and we don't want to. We want our own identity, and we are proud of the Jewish People. I am proud of being a member of the Jewish People and a citizen of the State of Israel.

But we are involved in a conflict that is going to go on for many years . . . the moment we set foot on this soil, each of us dispossessed an Arab.[5] When I was in my third year of National Service, I worked in a banana plantation with an Arab. This Arab . . . constantly remarked that we were working lands which had belonged to him and his family: . . . Many of us could tell similar stories.

We can't not be a free state and a free people. . . . But in the realisation of our justice, the Arabs are harmed. This is a fact. And as we have no alternative, we have to build up an army and fight. Our generation is going to be fighting for many years; we have already fought for many years for our justice, and there is no escaping it – but we must keep it clear in our minds that we are trampling the justice of others. That is why I think we are in some sort of tragic situation from which there is practically no way out.

Summary note of the author's talk with the same speaker, about a year later:

'In building the State and the Kibbutzim that generation forgot the spiritual objectives, and now this generation is faced with an essential and difficult search. The Shdemot group is engaged in that search and if they don't find an answer both the Kibbutzim and the State of Israel will break down.

'The war was a great crisis – the first time the young from the Kibbutzim fought and died. What for? It was no good going back to the old routine – winning wars and building fine Kibbutzim of itself gets you nowhere – without spiritual purpose it is spiritual failure.'

'The problem is not military survival. It is to find a new spirit, partly from the old tradition but with something new for this age. Tradition alone is not enough – we must find the connection between it and the new culture. If we fail, the Jews might as well return to other lands. Their work in Israel is to find a special culture, a special achievement. It must be something like Judaism because it is ours and we are its. Perhaps the answer may be found in a new social framework – like the Kibbutz. It is very difficult but we must try because it is our life.'

'Most young people', he went on, 'don't think about religion in the spiritual sense, but some do. They have an inner emptiness which isn't filled by work, production etc. Marxism has failed them. So they seek for a new spirit through the study of the Jewish religion. But they have no belief in "The Jewish God" nor in "praying". In their search for the "old Jewish culture" perhaps they will drink some spiritual living water from the well of culture.'

He is considering the study of sociology and psychology but isn't sure, and might turn to Jewish studies.

Before the war he was entirely indifferent to Judaism – it didn't matter. But the help of the Diaspora in money and people changed his and others' ideas, and they felt their Jewishness much more. He now feels strongly connected with Jews all over the world – if they 'cooled off' it would be very bad for Israel.

Another shortened extract from *Bein Zeirim*:

Ever since the war I've been trying to find an answer to the questions: Why do young boys have to die? And sometimes you find yourself not being able to help saying something like: Wouldn't you be ready to give the whole existence of the Jewish People in exchange for the lives of the fallen boys? . . . You might say: all nations fight for their homeland, for their natural

existence. . . . But the point is that throughout its history the
Jewish People has been surrounded by annihilation, threats to its
physical survival. Is there another nation that has to go on fighting
this way for its very life? . . . Not that tomorrow we're going to
pick ourselves up and pull out of here. That's not the point. The
problem is over justifying the war. How does a person persuade
himself to go into battle. Why? For what? What are we dying
for? Is it possible to give your life without knowing for what?

If I had been born in the Diaspora, maybe the whole thing
would be much clearer to me. My psychic makeup would be
different. I would have answers. The idea of living in this place as
a last haven, as the only solution for our national survival, would
be in my blood. But I was born here without the Jewish complex,
without . . . the Jewish justification, into a reality in which everybody hates me, surrounded by hatred, and I can't understand why,
what I've done to be ringed about by death and war?

Of course, from a dry rational standpoint, from the standpoint
of ideology, I understand the tragedy of the Jewish People . . . I
know that the only place for the Jew is Eretz Yisrael. Oh, I can
chant this refrain along with everybody – but . . . it doesn't
convince me. Everything that pertains to defending my life, the
lives of the people around me, my home – all this I feel. But I'm
not convinced about the business of defending the Jewish People
and the special reason for its existence.

The author's note of a talk a year or so later with the same speaker:

'The pioneers made a revolution; their children just learned
agriculture on the Kibbutz. We are so different we are almost not
Jews. Something is missing from my life: perhaps it is Judaism.'
He had been interested in religion from a child, but it was the
shock of war that roused him. He asked himself – why be killed
to be a Jew? What is this God of the Jews and what does he want
of us? So he went to the Jewish Theological Seminary's hostel in
Jerusalem for three days a week – a revolution for him. The
Kibbutz at first thought his wish to study religion 'frivolous', but
they saw his need and let him go. He doesn't know if study will
make him observant. It's very difficult on a secular Kibbutz, with
hardly another believer, and he doesn't yet positively want outward worship and observance. But if he wants to build a
synagogue, and can find five others, he is free to do so. 'Really to

be a Jew you must be in the widest sense religious. What is the
sense of all the "folklore" and "national culture"? The spiritual
sense of God is the central thing.'

An exchange from *Bein Zeirim*:

G. 'We had an ideological faith which I can say unequivocally has
collapsed almost completely. We believed in certain frameworks
which proved to be balloons. Today we're reconstructing our way.
We're putting ourselves back on our feet. And I have no clear
line today according to which I can educate my sons. . . . For me
general socialism was tied up with the Soviet Union. And that's
all gone for me . . .'
A. 'For you Jewishness is only a matter of inevitability, of fate,
and you feel a responsibility of fate. And it wouldn't matter to
you if you were a member of some Bedouin tribe near Kibbutz
Shuval: then you would maintain family ties with the tribe and
its ramifications, and you would be ready to give your life in the
tribe's wars, etc.'
G. 'I am a Jew by force: I was born a Jew.'
A. 'Can Judaism survive by force of destiny alone? Until about 80
years ago the reason for Jewish existence was mission, meaningful
existence. If you say survival, then I say meaningful survival.
Existence plus meaning. Now you say there is no meaning to the
existence of the Jewish People. All that remains, then, is Jewish
existence by heredity . . .'
B. 'There's no point getting involved in a discussion about the
meaning of the existence of the Jewish People. Where will that
get us? We're Jews, and there's no point debating that. The main
thing is to live. What's the difference what culture, which
tradition? There's no "justification" for the fact that I'm a Jew
rather than an Arab. It isn't a matter of logic.'
H. 'But I think that the main question is something else: because
the Jews lived with the special meaning of their existence without
a state. The question is whether we can live as a state without
meaning.'

Finally, extracts from a discussion on the subject of the Kibbutz
and Tradition, translated and condensed in *Petahim* (English edition),
September 1969.

A.G. 'Our generation finds itself now in a spiritual vacuum. In the

past we were in a certain sense deeply *religious*. We believed
religiously in world-revolution. . . . And now that faith has been
shattered. It is as if a religious Jew were lifted up to Heaven only
to find the throne of God empty.

'But it does not follow that the solution is to be found in
tradition. Tradition and religious faith are inseparable. Without
faith, the mere lighting of candles, etc., as an outward form is
valueless. And the trouble is that the secular education we received
is like an impenetrable glass screen, separating us from all contact
with Jewish thought and culture.

'Nevertheless, we must make an attempt to pierce the screen. . . .
One does not have to be "religious" (in the accepted sense) in order
to penetrate the screen.

'And we must begin from below – from our own children.
Why feed them only on Grimm's Tales or "Little Red Riding
Hood", when we have a wealth of tales, not less beautiful, in our
own literature? We should try to link each festival with Jewish
tradition and wisdom. We must educate our children – and ourselves first of all – to a love of Israel. Then perhaps the new
generation, now in the children's homes, may grow up with
Judaism, not as something stuck on outside, but as part of their
inner soul.

'There is no contradiction between Judaism and the kibbutz. On
the contrary unless we can integrate the kibbutz with Judaism –
then it will cease to maintain itself. But if we believe in the
possibility of such an integration, then there is a chance that our
own lives will be enriched and that the Kibbutz will remain
permanent.'

J.B. 'It is a mistake to suppose that there is no value in traditional
observances without "faith". On the contrary, the carrying out of
the observance may be a way of *approaching* faith . . . I recommend
a daily reading from the Bible, and from the book of Psalms in
particular . . . begin *at home* – i.e. in your own apartment, with
your children and perhaps a few friends, not in the dining-hall . . .'

A.Y. 'The founders of the kibbutz, although not "religious",
nevertheless had a deep *faith*, and that is what gave meaning to
their daily lives and to their festivals. Tradition must be regarded,
not as an occasional ornament, but as reflecting the ideals and
values which underlie our daily lives and human relations. The
Bar-Mitzvah, if it is merely the occasion for presents and a fat

meal, is worthless. Yom Kippur is more difficult. One may perhaps start in the home; but if the Kibbutz is not capable of a collective "reckoning" – what is the point of our being a Kibbutz? . . .'

In a later chapter we shall try to assess the meaning of these ideas and their implications for the future. Here we shall note the action being taken by those who express them. Their writings and seminars have been referred to. There are also more systematic forms of study. Some young people go to the University in Jerusalem or Tel Aviv, where their studies include a mixture of cultural and social subjects and 'Judaica'. A certain number each year attend classes and seminars at the Jewish Theological Seminary's hostel, maintained by the Conservative Judaism movement of America. This movement lays great emphasis on scholarship and in America systematically relates Jewish to secular learning: its New York seminary runs joint courses with Columbia University with mutual recognition for degree purposes. It sends a number of rabbinical trainees and other students for a year's study in Israel and associates local students with them, primarily for the American visitors' benefit but also for their own sake. The Israeli students are by no means all committed to religion. They include each year young secular Kibbutz members of the sort we have encountered. These meet, among their teachers and fellow students, men of a type unknown to them in Israel – orthodox or near-orthodox Jews with a fairly wide secular education, more advanced than their own, who can discuss religious questions with them in their own terms but with authority. There are such men in Israel but they are few, and if they wear the mantle of local orthodoxy they are put out of court by the Establishment's reputation as narrow and repressive in its approach. This may be the explanation for the otherwise extraordinary fact that there is little or no contact between the young seekers in search of religious meaning and the religious University of Bar-Ilan. There would seem however to be some opening here for initiative on either side.

Some American rabbis visit secular Kibbutzim for a few days' stay and are, they say, besieged by questioners who seem intrigued to meet men, and their families, of orthodox practice (as seen on Sabbath eve in the Kibbutz dining-hall) but broad educational equipment and cultured conversational style. Among the seminars in Jerusalem is one conducted by a disciple of Martin Buber. Buber's religious and ethical teaching has never had as much appeal within Israel as outside but it appears to hold considerable interest for some of the Kibbutzniks. It is impossible to guess how fruitful the whole marriage of American Jewish teaching with the secular Israeli desire for study may prove to be. Some observers in Israel doubt whether the approach of any American movement can be radical enough to achieve a permanent effect: perhaps not without some bias, they regard a form of Judaism which can content the secularized, half-assimilated Jewry of the West as unfit to deal with the sharp spiritual challenges that any 'modernized' religious life in Israel will have to meet. On the other hand other equally well-placed judges think that the best prospect for a religious revival in Israel is to be found here. It would not be the first time the Diaspora had led the way. Only the event can show.

Witness

7

Basis

Religious and secular agree on one fundamental proposition about the Jewish State which they share: its Jewish character must express itself in terms of social justice. Zionism, not in its essence a religious doctrine, shapes its aspirations by that ideal and has set out to realize it by specific performance. Religious Jews never forget the detailed, practical character of the Teaching by which they live. The prophetic vision is the soul of Judaism: the Talmud gave it body.

> The Judaism which ensured Jewish survival was supremely the religion of the 'know-how'. . . . The prophets denounced idolatry: the Pharisees developed the congregational worship of the synagogue. . . . The prophets proclaimed that the day should come when all men should know the Lord: the Pharisees intro-duced schools. . . . The prophets proclaimed that justice should run down like rivers: the rabbis examined the nature of evidence . . . and the technique of law courts. The prophets summoned all men to do righteously: the rabbis studied the wording of contracts.

The Jewish people have 'a perpetual analytic interest in how things work'.[1]

In this and the next four chapters we examine how things work; it is an essential aspect of the study of religion and nationalism, not here in confrontation but in their pragmatic interrelationships. We start with the broad political pattern.

It will throw some light on the unique character of public life in Israel if we begin by noting that its social-democratic character is of a most unusual kind: the 'left' resists nationalization and mistrusts central planning, while the 'right' – private enterprise and its political organs – actively favours both. This strange state of things is in fact the natural outcome of the original combination of British *laissez faire* colonial policy and the positive, purposive thrust of the early Zionist settlers.

At that time colonial policy – and not only British – was little concerned with constructive economic action in today's sense. 'Interventionism' was embryonic even in the domestic life of the colonial powers; in their colonial administrations it had scarcely been conceived. The Palestine Mandatory Government, which was much influenced by the character of British colonial policy, had the virtues of its tradition. It was very good at the business of government within the typical limits. It had a good record in law and justice, and its incorruptibility shone like a good deed in the Levantine murk. It had a policy for roads and railways, ports and harbours. But in face of a Jewish community with positive ideas of its own about production, education and health services, and with the will and energy to implement them, the Government was content to play a minor role, and confine its main attentions – limited in any case – to the needs of the Arabs. It raised taxes efficiently, spent a high proportion of them on 'law and order', and over the years remitted fairly large sums for investment in London. This did something to balance the increasing inflow of funds from Zionist sources. It was an odd kind of 'balance of payments', though no doubt it looked less so in the '20s and '30s. The Balfour Declaration's twin benedictions on the Jewish National Home and the rights of the non-Jewish inhabitants would each have been given more practical expression if more of the money raised in Palestine had been spent there.

The Zionist settlers however had their own ideas about building their community, and set about realizing their aims with exceptional thrust and persistence. They had their own means (Zionist funds), in a sense their own instruments (chiefly the Jewish National Fund and the Foundation Fund – Keren Hayesod) and their 'front' for dealing with both the Government and the outside world. This last was the Jewish Agency, set up for that purpose by the Government itself; and the World Zionist Organisation was recognized as the actual performer of the role. The settlers had imported with them not only a socialist ideology but also the Jewish proclivity for growth by self-division. Two Zionist socialist parties had been formed in the days of the Second Aliyah, one Marxist, one not. Each developed its 'labour wing'. They also founded some co-operative undertakings for production, distribution and medical insurance. Out of these grew in 1920 the General

Federation of Labour, the Histadrut (the word means organization) which can be set alongside the agricultural settlements as one of the two genuinely original institutional creations of pre-State Jewish Palestine.

Since all this was taking place not under the aegis of the Government nor with its money but by voluntary effort, and with overseas funds, the way was open for the exercise of that talent for faction to which we have referred. There was a multiplicity of parties to vote in the occasional elections for the Jewish representative assembly which the Government had set up. Most of these had an economic base: two were religious: one, the Revisionists (ancestor of the Herut half-party of today), had an aggressive, expansionist ideology aimed at a Jewish State including Trans-Jordan. The larger Left parties applied their constructive instincts independently of one another. Each had its own settlements, the Kibbutzim (with three separate groupings), and its own schemes of urban development. They and other parties also extended their activities further. They had, or came to have, not only housing projects, but loan societies, banks, health insurance and services, kindergartens, youth movements, sports clubs, publishing houses, Kibbutzim and Moshavim.

So there developed under the aloof, permissive policy of the Mandatory, a highly sectionalized economy and 'polity' in the Jewish community. This has marked it for good and ill to the present day. The independent government of Israel, when it came into being, found itself confronted by a collection of quasi-independent powers, performing many of the functions normally carried out by governments, especially social-democratic governments. These were a little like the barons of England in the days before the Crown finally asserted effective sovereignty, and like those 'over-mighty subjects' they owed their power chiefly to their command of the loyalties of a mass of dependents, who looked to them for benefits in such provinces as housing, insurance and employment opportunities. Before independence opened the floodgates, immigration permits had been among the chief levers of power and influence in the hands of parties and their sectional institutions. Both then and afterwards the entire structure was heavily buttressed by the system under which international moneys went to these sections in proportion to their numbers. This was an obvious incentive to acquire more members by any means available, and in this respect the apt comparison would not be with the English barons (who had to go to overt war to enlarge their estates) but with the ward politics of large American cities, where the inducements are mainly (not of course entirely) non-violent.

There is, however, a different way to read this story. Loyal Zionists speak of the underlying socialist solidarity of the great majority of settlers in the formative years, and of the way in which their broad purposes dovetailed with and supported those of the developing political organism of the '20s and '30s, and ultimately of the State itself. They also claim the superiority of that form of social democracy which attaches less weight to nationalization by the State than do inferior kinds like the British, and troubles less about winning a commanding political position than about achieving possession of the commanding heights of the economy by building them up oneself. One may take this view as an ideological gloss on historical accident and hard political fact, or as an insight that penetrates below the rather gritty surface to the inward truth about Israel's domestic polity. There is more common ground than this might suggest between the two interpretations. One cannot explain the astonishing achievements of the pioneers, however sectional their methods, apart from their socio-nationalist convictions and the sustained effort of nerve and will and applied intelligence which these inspired.

To return from interpretation to hard fact: the workers' movement has a membership of one million and is, in its tiny State, the eighth largest of its kind in the world. It has been in power for nearly forty years, if we include its dominant position in the national assembly before the State was founded. Its economic predominance, as owner and employer, is the single most important fact about Israel's domestic economy. The Histadrut, directly and through its subsidiaries and affiliates, employs about nine tenths of the wage- and salary-earners in the country,[2] and it accounts for a fifth to a quarter of the domestic product. Its empire (or fief) includes heavy industries, transport, buildings, marketing and retail business, agricultural settlements, dramatic companies and an orchestra. Besides the intangible social and political benefits carried by membership of so large and powerful an organization it provides its members with educational, cultural, housing and social services, notably a fairly comprehensive medical insurance scheme, to which the labour organizations of the two religious parties are affiliated. It has successfully recruited and accepts on equal terms a large Arab membership, perhaps a quarter to a third of the whole Arab labour force in Israel proper: its policies made inevitable the payment of the same wages to Jewish and Arab Israelis.

The savings of its members through their pension and insurance funds go to finance more worker-owned enterprises or extend present ones. Politically, it is controlled by Mapai, the Israel Labour Party, which is both the dominant partner in successive coalition governments and holder of a permanent majority in the Histadrut's elective Convention, nominator of its executive bodies.

An integral relation of this kind, based as it obviously is on a shared political philosophy between the leading political party and the most powerful economic force in the State, is of great value to both. This was what underpinned the structure of the unofficial governments before the State was formed, and enabled Ben-Gurion to take over as a going concern a working political machine. It could even hand over to the State the Hagana, the Citizen Army, which had its headquarters in the Histadrut's executive offices. The broad identity of its purposes with those of the State means, for example, that Israel has no vested interest of workers against unrestricted immigration, and that labour relations are well above average in quality.

There is of course a price to be paid for all this – some of it obvious, some not so much so. The Israel Labour Movement is against the idea of a National Health service: it has its own, which does not include the small self-employed, shopkeepers etc., who may need it. Its incomes policy, not unnaturally, takes a more generous view of desirable wage levels than an unfettered central government might do, and its own practices as an employer enforce upon other employers standards of payment that may not suit them and – they argue – do not suit the real interests of the economy. These are typical reasons why private business and its political spokesmen want more planning, more nationalization, more central control of the economy. In other countries the Left wants governments that will keep private business in order so as to see fair play for the workers. In Israel, the Right looks to central authority to keep the dominant labour-owned public sector within bounds. The 'underprivileged' or those who feel so are always prone to call the Sovereign to their rescue.

There are more subtle dangers too. The Histadrut is one part – a very powerful and important part – of a politico-economic system that rests upon entrenched groupings wielding political, economic and social influence. The combination of underlying solidarity and fierce sectionalism found its natural outcome in a system of proportional representation whose effect has been to furnish Israel with what must be the least removable government in any democracy. The Scandinavians

97

are volatile by comparison. The same party grouping, with a few fringe variations, has sat in power for decades. The average Knesset and Cabinet member is not young, and is getting steadily less so. The parties are locked into a system of mutual pressures which cannot but substitute party deals for true political decision. The examples noted in earlier chapters from the secular-religious sphere could be multiplied in others. The various Ministries themselves go in large part and by prior arrangement to particular parties, which limits the Prime Minister's patronage and authority, and the flexibility of choice that goes with it. Most of the Ministries, moreover, (and the parties that 'own' them) carry their own types of patronage: they have contracts to place, permits to grant, jobs to allot. When one adds this to the allocation of international Zionist funds to parties and their institutions under the system already mentioned, one understands why one of the commonest 'Hebrew' words the foreigner overhears in Israel is the 'Russian' word 'protectzia', which represents, *anglice*, a combination of the old-boy network and plain political pull.

If the point is being laboured it is for a reason. The intelligent young are bitterly alienated by this sort of politics: it is a threat to the quality of life: it offends and repels them. Since they mistrust and will have no part of it, they turn their back on issues of great moment to themselves and their country, on which they have points of view that should be heard. In one of the author's conversations with able young Kibbutzniks, referred to in Chapter 6, one of them said that the question of the Arab refugees from the Six-Day War could have been solved 'if we had really tried'. Asked why he himself did not make some move accordingly he said: 'That's politics and when you're in politics you're in trouble.' He has – as have many others – a raw and vivid memory of the traumatic split in the Kibbutz movement twenty years ago, on political grounds in a very unhappy sense of that phrase, and he is unready to face the inevitable threat to his own integrity that political involvement seems to him to carry. A country as small as Israel, so new to the responsibilities of State power, under so many fierce pressures, can hardly afford this sort of alienation. It may be more dangerous than the crudities of the New Left.

What makes the present political rigidity even more dangerous is the contrast between it and the radical changes that are under way in society and the economy. In its beginnings, Israel was an idealist society practising a form of Utopian socialism on the land and an egalitarian semi-collectivism over much of its industry and distribution. Under influences common to it and other advanced economies, it is moving from Utopian ideals to the practical problems of exploiting scientific advances and new technologies. On the land, once the special focus of idealism, fewer people are now producing more; there are more of them to spare for industry, which is offering them more chances. Military needs, new technical opportunities, business talent in quest of an outlet, have combined to shift the balance of the economy more and more towards industrial production. Around Tel-Aviv and in other urban areas, but also in a growing number of Kibbutzim and Moshavim, industry is developing, some of it on high technical levels. Israel is obviously well qualified to exploit advanced technology, but the present onset of this, and its evident future prospects, both call for an attitude towards education that must clash with the conventional ideology of the community on three different fronts.

One is in the Kibbutz, as a later chapter will show. Another is in the province of orthodox religious education, in the religious State schools, where the interest and opportunity offered by secular careers will with some young people tell against the present heavy concentration on religious subjects: it seems probable that a fraction at least, enough to make a difference, will come to resent a system in which secular contemporaries of equal ability out-distance them over an increasing range of productive and distributive activity, because they are better educated for the new world. The third area of conflict is in the bureaucratic hierarchies of the State, the local authorities, the Histadrut and the other collectives in industry and commerce. Here salaries are on scales easier to justify by egalitarian than normal economic principles. The 'steps' are not wide: seniority counts for a good deal: social need (large families) is recognized by a system of allowances. Altogether the younger men have a good deal less personal incentive to seek high qualifications than their opposite numbers even in the more egalitarian democracies of the West. There is already some shortage of special skills; it may be made good in part by the increasing intake of qualified people from Western countries[3] but unless this greatly accelerates it is unlikely to fill the gap.

There is no need to carry speculation too far. Plainly the priorities of an advanced technological community are not those of the pioneers, and some hard political choices lie ahead. The argument has in fact started already. The typical 'Labour Zionist' looks at the large proportion of really poor people in the State (estimated at 300,000 who depend on public funds in some form) and demands priority for their needs.

On the other hand some of those possessing the special skills that are in short supply argue that the present gap between the pay of 'technocrats' and of the sub-average worker is too narrow and needs to be widened in the general interest. That the economic future of Israel may depend on the planned exploitation of the special qualities of her most gifted citizens, is a thesis argued by Arie L. Eliav, a Deputy Minister, in an imaginative brochure *New Targets for Israel*, which has attracted a great deal of interest. Surprisingly, however, it does not discuss the implications for economic policy, or egalitarian principles, of a technocratic society built on the increasing exploitation of Israel's special assets of brainpower and advanced education. Here is one of the cruxes in all advanced economies. If the special values of life in the Jewish State are to prove themselves in this uncommonly difficult field, it is not too soon for imaginative thinkers at least to give the issues an airing.

8

Two Pillars

(i) THE ARMY

Among the first and greatest achievements of the newly independent State was to centralize and democratize military authority. During the formative years before independence, with the world war raging and struggle with the Arabs and the British impending, the typical sectionalism of the Jewish community showed itself in three separate military organizations. After power struggles and one direct military confrontation, Ben-Gurion dissolved two of the headquarters and integrated all voluntary command structures in one military establishment, based on universal compulsion and under full State control. It took some years to integrate also the ideological impulses behind the three original fighting forces and to establish the supremacy of military over political aims. This was a considerable feat of statesmanship and a witness to the spirit of the community. What emerged was a unique citizen army, in which the ethical and political aims of the people were preserved alive, along with, though subordinate to, the overriding purposes of effective defence. The Army was freed from the almost all-pervading 'politicization' of public life and government, in the sense that party interests and sectional objectives played no significant part in its conduct. Like any democratic army it has an interest in ensuring that security enjoys due priority among the political aims of the State. Its success in this, however, has rested not on behind-the-scenes influence but on widespread public support.

There is nevertheless a sense, beneficent and constructive, in which it has remained a thoroughly political instrument. It has been deliberately employed to inculcate, protect and extend the civic culture and values of the national State. When the Commander of Israel's victorious army returned thanks for his honorary degree (the nation's first honour to its conquering hero, almost on the morrow of his triumph, was to make him a Doctor of Philosophy!) Major-General Rabin said: 'What is there in common between those whose profession is violence and those who are concerned with spiritual values? . . . The world has recognized that the Israel Army is different from other armies. Although its first task is the military one of maintaining security, it has numerous peace-time roles, not of destruction but of construction and of strengthening the nation's cultural and moral resources.'[1]

It performs these tasks in an atmosphere of almost universal support for, and pride in, its military but also its civil role. It does a great deal to 'stretch' its soldiers by expecting the utmost of them and training them to expect it of themselves. The concept of leadership for which it trains suitable young men and women includes the duties of citizenship as well as those of battle.

> Such values as developing the soldier's self-respect and moving him to voluntary co-operation, development of his national consciousness, encouragement of his social ability, and even more basic values such as speaking truth, seeking justice, loving peace and holding human life sacred, are regarded by the Defence Forces as extremely relevant, both to combat and to general humanistic education.[2]

It plays a special role as forcing-house in which recruits from the Afro-Asian communities can make up educational leeway. Those who could not finish with elementary school before call-up are sent for intensive teaching, in a special school, working long hours in classes of ten, each with two teachers. There are correspondence courses and special classes to encourage soldiers to finish high-school studies, and a one-year course to prepare for higher education. This is part of their military service and the aim is to send them to speed up the progress of backward communities, handicapped socially by their backgrounds. Their success rate is over 90 per cent compared with a general average of 5 per cent.

The Army's role extends beyond the stretching and upgrading of its own people to direct attacks on communal problems – agricultural development, adult illiteracy, backward schools in remote or isolated towns and districts. (A substantial fraction of the women recruits are assigned to teaching work.) There is also the work of Nahal. This is a pioneer corps trained not only for special military tasks such as commando work, but also for intensive farming on newly founded settlements in exposed areas. Its units may be sent to backward or problem towns and villages to teach, set up clubs, arrange adult courses, and tackle social difficulties among poor or handicapped families.

In all this can be seen, deliberately applied, the special *ethos* of the State of Israel, the socialist-Zionist creed that holds sway widely over religious and secular alike. It is clearly related to the basic ethical values of Judaism. The Army's social and educational work is one part of the witness. The spirit in which it tackles its military duties is another, and this affinity with the tradition is more profound than the spirit of the tribal warrior – 'The sword of the Lord and of Gideon'. As General Rabin put it, in the immediate aftermath of the war,

> A strange phenomenon can be observed among our soldiers. Their joy is incomplete, and their celebrations are marred by sorrow and shock. . . . The men in the front lines saw with their own eyes not only the glory of victory but also the price of victory – their comrades fallen beside them soaked in blood. I know too that the terrible price paid by our enemies also touched the hearts of many of our men. It may be that the Jewish people has never learned and never accustomed itself to feel the triumph of conquest and victory, with the result that these are accepted with mixed feelings.

One hears the note of some of the young speakers in *The Seventh Day*: 'It is these visions [of the horrors of persecution] which compel us to fight and yet make us ashamed of our fighting.'

(ii) THE KIBBUTZ

If secular Judaism has in Israel one outstanding civilian institution to witness to its character and the nature of its achievement, it is the collective agricultural settlement, the Kibbutz. Modern history is littered with the ruins of other experiments in Utopian socialism. The Kibbutz has survived for over half a century and is still vigorously alive. It is possibly the only secular institution in Israel that has been flattered by imitation from the religious side. There are about twelve religious Kibbutzim of a total of about 230. The overwhelming majority are secular in origin and spirit. It is with them that this chapter is concerned.

There were some specific reasons why the men and women of the Second Aliyah banded together collectively on the land. On the land, because of the longing of the children of the ghetto for the rounded fulfilment it offered, and the mystique this longing bred: but also because there was then no capital for urban development or the foundation of industries. Collectively, because that was the spirit of the crusading idealism that set out to build model socialist communities: but also for security against marauding or resentful Arabs, and to ensure year-long employment for raw recruits from the ghetto who could not have matched the productive capacity of hired Arab labour. The real underlying explanation was certainly ideological. Nothing but the fervour of Jewish nationalist and socialist convictions could have carried the pioneers through, and this was what gave the Kibbutz both its life and its soul. The secret of these convictions, the peculiar Jewish ingredient, was their ethical impulse, the ingrained feeling for social justice practically expressed. The Mosaic laws and the prophetic teaching had etched these so deeply on Jewish minds that the pattern was little blurred by secular colouration. Moshe Kerem, one of the founders of a secular Kibbutz, wrote in an interview in *Petahim*:

> If one considers the spirit of Judaism, that is those deep spiritual values which govern men's behaviour towards one another, then I have no doubt that it is preserved in the Kibbutz as much as it has ever been elsewhere, and furthermore, that it is preserved in an essentially Jewish way, namely in a community.

Five years after the Mandate began, there were less than a score of Kibbutzim, with an average of 60 inhabitants. By the outbreak of the world war there were about 50, by the end of it well over 100, with an average population around 350. Today the Kibbutz population is 3–4 per cent of that of Israel. Throughout the period the Kibbutz has made special and positive contributions to the life of the community and the security of the State – absorbing into its ready-made community life a large number of immigrants from Europe, responding to the national need to extend settlement into the toughest and remotest areas, setting up quasi-military frontier outposts.

Its peculiar features are well enough known to require no more than a summary reminder. Its economy is fully collective, all its land, buildings and other capital being held in common. Income is pooled, and allotted to individuals by central decision according to need. Work is allotted similarly; there is little or no feeling of occupational status and no incentive system of money payment. Administration is by a central and various functional elective committees, with a general assembly, usually weekly, in final control. There is equality of the

sexes though in practice women were restricted, at least until fairly
recently, to the traditional callings. Family life is partly communal:
parents have their separate dwellings and mostly eat in the central
dining hall. They see their children for a few hours in the afternoon.
This is beginning to change but still, in most Kibbutzim, the children
sleep, eat and of course learn in their own quarters. This, say the
apologists, gives the children the benefit of superior professional care,
enables the mothers to work without family distractions, and frees
the relation of husband and wife from the extraneous and sometimes
debasing influence of economic bonds.

The economic results do not discredit the effectiveness of these
Utopian ideas. Starting from a life-standard of extreme austerity, the
older settlements have reached one of very fair middle-class comfort,
based on high technical efficiency. Morally, some were among the first
to adopt the permissive attitudes now common in Western countries,
with – on some Kibbutzim – complicated effects on the relation
between biological lines of descent and the visible composition of
families. Socially, they gave an unquestionable lead. Norman Bentwich has written that in the mandatory period they were 'the conscience of the nation', and many would say they still are. They are
often described as the national élite: certainly they have far more than
their proportionate share of war casualties, army commissions, and
seats in the Knesset and the Cabinet. A Minister evidently expects the
same sort of political bonus from membership of a Kibbutz, where he
spends weekends and waits at table like an ordinary mortal, as his
British counterpart would once have gained from delivering lay
sermons in church or playing cricket for his county. The moral leadership of the Kibbutz is, however, now being questioned by some
observers whose inquiries, they say, show that among young people
in the cities who make up a large segment of the population the
priority scale of values has changed in recent years, with the Army,
diplomacy and the higher bureaucracy displacing the Kibbutz which is
now low on the list. Public opinion on a point like this is not only hard
to measure but apt to shift back and forth. For the longer term, a safer
guide to the extent of Kibbutz leadership may be to consider whether
it deserves to lead, as reckoned by standards of performance that public
opinion in Israel would itself accept as valid.

There is some firm evidence about the superiority of young Kibbutzniks in military potential. An academic specialist in social psychology,
who was for four years head of the Psychological Research Institute of

the Israel Armed Forces, has made a study whose findings are genuinely interesting and on their face convincing. Three comparable groups of soldiers were measured against one another: those born on Kibbutzim, those who entered them before they were ten, and the others. They were tested first for the personal qualities they brought into the army with them. The Kibbutz-born were ranked 'conspicuously superior to the other two groups' in intelligence as normally measured. Education-ally, more than four out of five reach a high level, with hardly any of them in the two lowest brackets. Tests of personality, in those aspects which the army reckons relevant to its needs, make the Kibbutz-born 'superior to all the rest of the population in their personality rating'. Much of this can be related to the fact that the Kibbutz-born were *ipso facto* born in Israel, as compared with a little over a third of the other groups, whose average standards are lowered by the severe social and economic handicaps still suffered by those of Afro-Asian back-ground, now about half the general population. This may explain but it does not alter the facts of Kibbutz superiority.

Military efficiency was reckoned by three standards – readiness to volunteer, achievement of promotion and success in officers' training schools.

The first standard covered both the extent of volunteering and the fighting requirements of the units chosen. Thirty per cent of the Kibbutz-born were placed in the highest of three groups, 19 per cent of the Kibbutz-bred, 5 per cent of the others. In the score-table of 'suitability for command positions' 61 per cent of the Kibbutz-born were in the top group, 40 of the Kibbutz-bred, 39 of the others. In the officers' school, 88 per cent of the Kibbutz-born passed, 75 per cent of the others. (The narrower margin here is thought by some analysts of this report to be related to the fact that, because of their numbers, the soldiers from outside the Kibbutzim were subject to a much more stringent entrance test.)

Finally, some statistical adjustments were made to enable comparisons to be made between Kibbutz-born and others of Israeli birth and good education. The same general superiority of the 'true' Kibbutzniks emerged. As the report puts it, 'when personal characteristics are held constant [i.e. eliminated from the comparisons] the difference between the three sub-groups shrinks but does not disappear . . . the Kibbutz-born continue to be superior to the rest of the population.' Even the shrinkage would seem to be an illusion since the personal characteristics whose effect has been discounted are themselves partly related to 'factors

inherent in the structure of the Kibbutz'. To prove that the achievements thus tested are a genuine measure of soldierly quality, one may
round off this picture by introducing a fact of another kind. The
Kibbutz population is about 4 per cent of the State's total. The
Kibbutz fighters killed in the Six-Day War were 25 per cent of the
total.

In its tentative search for explanations, the report looks in two
directions. One is towards the Kibbutz regime: child-rearing, the
special educational system, the inculcated drive towards achievement.
These are integral to Kibbutz life. The other is towards effects regarded
as a present by-product of that life but capable of achievement by other
means: the high level of nursing and teaching staff, better hygiene,
food and housing, and the powerful effect on the young man of the
expectation of his own Kibbutz and of all Israelis that he will do well in
military service. It is not apparent how this important one differs from
the last-mentioned of the 'integral' effects. The most interesting general
hypothesis that emerges in the mind of the writer of the report is that
the Kibbutz environment, training and education promote 'the
children's emotional development towards personal autonomy' – an
intriguing outcome of the collective system. The outside observer can
provide some slight confirmation in his awareness of the notable
readiness and ability of the typical Kibbutznik to speak his mind
plainly on any subject. The subject of 'personal autonomy', or its roots
in the Kibbutz, is under further study by the author[3] of the document
which we have summarized.

The criteria used in the military test from which the Kibbutz emerges
with so much credit were not too far removed from those most
obviously appropriate to its special aim of self-discipline and austerity.
The tests imposed on it by radical change in the economy and in the
pattern and values of civilian life might prove more severe and their
outcome more uncertain. Work on the land, which used to have
something of missionary quality and was looked up to accordingly,
now enjoys much lower prestige, and is done in large part by the
newer immigrants whose feet are still on the lower rungs of the social
ladder. These immigrants themselves, whose absorption has been the
most demanding of all civilian tasks since Independence, are not well
suited to the life of the Kibbutzim, whose contribution to this key
problem has lagged noticeably. (This is in the nature of things: by way
of typical example there was a group of Cochin Jews settled on a large
secular Kibbutz in the mid-'50s. The patriarchs from Asia could not

square it with their ideas of family life that their wives should do work as responsible as their own and be as well paid for it or, if they won some seniority, even better. They dispersed to more congenial life in the co-operative villages or to routine jobs in the towns, where in their separate households they could adjust at their own pace to the unheard-of values of Israeli life.) The pressures of urban life, the growth of industry, the progress of technology with its demand for advanced academic qualifications, all clashed with the standards of the Kibbutz. How has it dealt with the challenges of the managerial revolution?

The development of industry on the Kibbutzim began in fact some dozen years ago, with light and not very advanced forms of production. These called for the employment of some labour from outside. The distaste felt for the idea of 'hired help' was one reason why Kibbutz authorities have sought for more developed, capital-intensive kinds of production, with less need for labour. Another reason was that a higher yield per man was needed to realize higher material expectations, given the fulfilment of these in the cities. It was no part of Kibbutz ideology to allow themselves to become economic back-waters, especially since their comparatively high standards of education qualified them for positions in the van rather than the rear of Israel's advancing labour force. The same qualities as were reflected in the military tests endowed the Kibbutz with an exceptional reserve of good managerial talent. This is based as we have seen partly on an almost universally 'European' background. But again, the boys on the Kibbutzim have thirteen years of education (girls a little less) compared with a national average of nine years for males. The habit of devotion to an idea and the directly felt relation between effort and group reward are powerful incentives, which result in labour costs distinctly lower than those of employed workers. There is also an underlying bias towards the idea of high technology, created and fostered by the highly efficient agricultural techniques in which the settlements take pride.

Tentative comparisons of Kibbutz farming with that of the whole population show a 30–40 per cent greater efficiency per man, and a return on capital more than 50 above the general average. These figures are no accident of fortune: they apply equally to irrigated and non-irrigable land, and it would be surprising if they were not matched also in industrial production. Here too the output of the Kibbutzim competes in the open markets at home and abroad, and the speed of their industrial growth and extension is proof of efficiency. Economic studies by the Falk Institute (Jerusalem) show that the share of Kibbutz capital that is invested in industry, originally very small, is now about 35 per cent and that the growth in this proportion is accelerating. Industrial production already accounts for at least 40 per cent, very likely more, of Kibbutz income.

These changes have created their own problems and have called for radical change in the way production is organized. Agricultural efficiency requires specialization, but when specialist managers lay down technical methods and work norms they cut across older ideas of autonomous working by individuals or small groups. Moreover, industrial efficiency needs not only managerial skill, but a labour force that accepts discipline on the job. In the West, industry is based on the assumption of discipline: the problem is to achieve 'participation' by those engaged. On the Kibbutz, participation is the starting point and discipline the goal. That is the easier objective and on the whole it is attained. Given the sense of common purpose it is not difficult to win assent to practical standards and a hierarchical structure. There are obvious risks that leaders in the factory will seek, or be half-consciously accorded, a status as leaders in the society: that specialist managers will acquire a sort of title to particular functions; that good performers in industry or on the farms will be frozen in their jobs; most dangerous of all, that the technocrats as a body will escape the democratic control of the Kibbutz organs of government – the various committees – or worse still will begin to dominate them. The risk of replacing democracy by technocracy has not escaped notice, and in the livelier settlements corrective steps have been taken. Supervision has been split up far enough to ensure that the elective committees can stay close to their charges. There is rotation in work and in range of managerial responsibility. There are special measures for checking and control by committees, and for effective reporting to the central assembly, the general meeting of the Kibbutz. In such ways the spirit of the Kibbutz expresses itself; to think of them as mere 'nuts-and-bolts problems' is to overlook the practical spirit of Judaism itself, and perhaps to miss a possible analogy with the down-to-earth way the Rabbis of the classical period 1,900 years ago set about applying the spirit of the prophetic message to the problems posed by daily life and its changes. On some highly secular Kibbutzim this comparison might be thought a good joke: it could still contain some truth.

The Kibbutzim are, on the whole, well supplied with people of managerial calibre and the capacity to lead. Indeed there is an oversupply, and this creates a problem. A partial solution is found by 'going out to work' – taking part-time jobs of suitable calibre in public or private establishments. This in turn makes problems: the social life of the Kibbutz was founded on close proximity all round and if the husband or father is there only at weekends it leaves a gap and creates tensions, which his outside earnings (paid to the Kibbutz) do not directly lessen.

A more deep-seated difficulty concerns higher education. Up to the final secondary school (high school) year provision for the education of Kibbutz children is unmatched. But the special qualifications demanded by modern industry or sought by aspiring teenagers involve a demand for higher education which the founding fathers frowned upon. They had turned their backs on their own professional or academic pasts in favour of what they felt to be a higher calling and they expected their offspring to be equally content with Kibbutz life and values. Recognition that this point of view does not fit aptly into the contemporary world of high technology and universal intercommunication has come slowly and with some difficulties. Even on purely practical grounds, adding three years at a university or college to three years of military service (two years for unmarried girls) makes a big hole in the productive life of the young. But time and the thrust of youth increasingly have their way.

It is the conflict of the generations thus exemplified that has perhaps presented the Kibbutzim with their greatest task of adjustment. The Kibbutz has its own traditional ideas, and there are clashes between the new shoots and the 'crust of custom'. The pioneers were revolutionaries who brought a world-experience to focus on their newly created form of life. The next generation finds its world ready-made. It looks about, and out; conscious of its parents' background, it is not content.

The differences take many forms, the simplest and most obvious being the usual argument about who is to run things. Are the old hanging on too long, or are the young trying to run before they can walk? Or again, and also not confined to Kibbutzim or to Israel, have the old realized these ideals fully enough to justify their prescribing them to the young? The answer to such a question is almost inevitably 'No' in any society at any time, since man's reach exceeds his grasp and the old have only what they have grasped while the young see only what they expect to reach. But in Israel this issue takes a peculiarly sharp and sometimes painful form. Kibbutz society was founded on an ideal and the older generation founded it. It was an exacting, almost other-wordly ideal, to which they were ready to sacrifice the more personal, the gentler aspects of life. The young were born into an easier environment, a country won for them, and a world in which a little self-indulgence seems less culpable and self-realization a positive good. They are conscious of their elders' failures and shortcomings. They challenge the whole approach that would put ideas and institutions before people, norms before insights, the collective before the individual. The pendulum is swinging, more than a little.

On the secular Kibbutzim, the religious approach does not seem to play any significant part in these particular wrestlings. The Tradition takes purely cultural, that is to say secular, forms nearly everywhere. The festivals are kept, and highly valued for their colour and gaiety. The young children are inducted in their kindergartens into this pattern of ceremonial and these simple rituals. On many secular Kibbutzim – by no means all – they see the Sabbath candles lit in the communal dining hall, and a special meal laid. Seder service, on the first eve of Passover, is read in something like the immemorial form, stripped now of the topical versions and vagaries that were common a few years ago. How far this return towards conformity is because of the special contemporary relevance of the Festival of Deliverance, how far because this has always been the best-loved of festivals and its power over the Jewish imagination greatest, one cannot guess. Nor can one be sure that beneath these levels of habitual cultural activity there may not be some remnant of pious feeling, some spark which the ashes of past faith both hide and preserve. As we have seen, a few score individuals scattered among the secular settlements show evidence of interest in religious experience and are active in its pursuit. But of any general awareness of transcendent spiritual power, of any overt acceptance of ethical standards because they reflect or express that power, there appear to be no signs.

The question with which we are mainly concerned at this point is the vitality of the Kibbutz as a secular institution, whatever implication that may have for the vitality of Judaism itself. The main favourable evidence is the fact that the ideas and values of the Kibbutz, however defined, have shown themselves capable of standing up to new circumstances, and dealing effectively with challenges beyond the imagination of the founders. When Kibbutz industry started it was regarded by nearly everyone as a sign of debasement and decline. Now it is seen as a new shoot from an established root, one which, like this year's new growth of a young climbing rose, may well turn out to dwarf its predecessors and alter the whole pattern displayed. Any advanced society is nowadays compelled to realize that industry cannot be efficiently run against the resistance or even the apathy of the workers. The British Minister in charge of Employment and Productivity, Barbara Castle, said as much in 1969: 'We have got to recognize, whether we like it or not, that real power now resides in the workshop and on the office floor. It has, if you like, returned to the grass roots whence it came. We have got to accept, again whether we like it or not, that workpeople have a veto which they are increasingly prepared to exercise; in other words, that management these days can no longer function by the arbitrary exercise of traditional "prerogatives", but only by winning the consent of its workpeople.' What the Kibbutz has is a basis of consent. It has no serious labour problems, not because the machinery of industrial relations is well-planned (though it is not neglected) but because the awareness of common purpose is stronger than sectional difference. It can compete with private industry, which indeed sometimes farms out to Kibbutzim some of its processes, especially those calling for special ability. The more alert and progressive of the settlements look for new technological developments which they can either sell to industry under licence or exploit themselves: in this quest some of them bring in scientists of high calibre from the academic field. All this is a long way from the earlier inward look, and is a particular sign of the power of growth.

There are some developments on the social side as well. The earlier doctrinaire policies on family life are softening. In older Kibbutzim the children spend more time at home: in some newer ones they live with their parents, in an overall pattern of life and work not very different from one kind of co-operative village. The use of the Kibbutz as a domestic base for an outside job has been referred to. What started as a movement from the Kibbutz outwards is continuing in the reverse direction. People with jobs elsewhere look for a personal home and stake in the Kibbutz; more than that, some settlements are setting out to attract this type of recruit, especially from among those with high professional qualifications. In 1970 an agency called the Centre for Directing People to Development Towns and Settlements arranged with the Kibbutz organizations that it should begin an advertising campaign: 'The Kibbutz offers you a home. Kibbutzim are developing: new Kibbutzim are going up; over 200 veteran and new Kibbutzim and settlements, in all parts of the country, appeal to you to join them.'

The head of this Centre is reported as saying that they expect to attract, and are attracting, people long settled in the country who will continue in their professional callings; they will no longer be put, as newcomers have been, at the tail of the queue for better-grade housing but will be provided with something better from the start.

Such changes provide a clue to the next phase in the development of the Kibbutz. This is indeed already upon them and is exercising the minds of the younger generation about its implications for their communal homes and their own lives. So far, the Kibbutz idea is not threatened. The great majority stay on their settlement or come back to it. The influence of the family as guardian of stability and continuity remains powerful. But the more profoundly reflective among the rising generation believe that the question that matters most is whether they will continue to keep alive the sense of mission which launched and has sustained them. What would become of an awareness of common purpose if the purpose was no more than to raise the material and cultural levels of Kibbutz life, and to provide individual members with better opportunities for personal fulfilment? A renewal of mission may be found partly in the future development of a constructive relation between the Kibbutz and the community as a whole. The whole question, however, may raise deeper issues about the limits of secular living and thinking. In a Jewish community, even if many of its members have moved far from the ancestral anchorage, it would be strange if the values of humanism continued to provide the whole framework of thought and discussion. Indeed it is clear already that an active minority would not be content to have them do so.

The collective settlements could, in theory, cut themselves off from any but impersonal economic relations with the rest of the community, as little cells of comfort exploiting their practical capacities for their own exclusive sakes. This is so out of character as to be hard to credit, and the pointers to the future that are already available make it an even more improbable outcome. It is not unreasonable to envisage the Kibbutz developing wider and more constructive relations with the community, maintaining its prestige by fresh achievement, exerting a continued leadership by example – by the practical force of visibly effective ideas and methods. What Israel, like other free democratic communities, requires over the whole field of its corporate life, are means for relating individual effort to common purposes, incentives that work without fostering greed and selfishness. These are what the Kibbutz shows some prospect of demonstrating. It would be perverse to deny any connection between them and the ethical values of Judaism from which their initial impulse derived. Whether these values could stay alive and in full expression if they were cut off from the original spiritual root is a question beyond the limits of this chapter. It raises again, in new and topical form, the inescapable question of the true nature of Judaism.

9

Ingathering

in 1948, 650,000

At Independence the Jews in Israel numbered about 650,000. A high proportion were of European, American or local birth or descent. After the 1948 war the wrath of the Arab countries fell on their Jewish citizens, the defenceless kinsmen of their enemies. In the years between 1949 and 1956 about 390,000 African and Asian Jews migrated *massive* to Israel, and in the next eleven years, up to 1967, another 216,000 *influx of* arrived. Western immigration in the same two periods amounted to 470,000. The 600,000 'coloured' Jews – all shades to full black – were *Afro-1* of no uniform cultural level: they ranged from the Yemenis and the *Asian* Kurds, living much as they had done for centuries, through semi-sophisticated townsmen from Morocco, to some professional people *Jews,* from Cairo or Beirut. But in the main they were alien in background *post* and culture, a century or two behind in their levels of technique and *1948* accompanying modes of thought, with oriental ideas of family life and the position of women. Very few spoke Hebrew.

The newcomers had to be taken in, housed, fed and employed, with massive international help, but by a community already intensely preoccupied, and spending around a third of its budget on defence. Nor were these the most serious problems. The immigrants, like all such groups, tended to segregate themselves and to be cut off by the formidable gap in education and social habit between them and their neighbours. Before long there was talk of 'the two communities' and even – unsuitably – 'a wasp-and-wog situation'. This was an offence to the *ethos* of the State, a bad smell in Zionist nostrils. At first the official reaction was to ignore it, not merely in the hope that it would cure itself but because official cognizance would seem to imply a sort of recognition of this glaring inequality in the egalitarian community. (In the same way, British authorities would not keep separate housing statistics for coloured Commonwealth immigrants; the omission obstructed needful remedial policies but to seek the information seemed too invidious.) There was also some well-meaning sentiment about the values of separate cultures, the need to preserve them, and the danger of assuming Western superiority.

As time went on, however, it became plain that the social chasm was growing wider and deeper; the great inequality of performance in elementary schools led to a far greater disparity in the numbers receiving secondary education, and then by a sort of geometrical progression to one still wider in higher education. In the mid-'60s, official statistics showed that children born in the West had a sevenfold better chance of getting higher education than those born in Africa or Asia, and that children born in Israel of 'Western' parents again did nearly seven times as well, by this reckoning, as Sabras whose fathers were Afro-Asian. Worse still, in a sense, the figures showed that these *Israel-born* Afro-Asians, though they did twice as well as immigrant children of the same origin, still lagged far behind *immigrant* children from the West; in other words one generation of exposure to Israeli life and conditions did so little to close the gap that at the same rates of change it would take nearly a century to achieve an integrated community. This sort of time scale is far too long both for the objective needs of the community and for its cultural aspirations.

Yet more. One of the normal signs of educational and social inferiority is a higher reproduction rate. The Afro-Asian share of the Israeli population has in fact been rising. This growing disproportion enlarges the problem. It makes levelling up in the schools far harder, and deprives the State of the full percentage of highly trained men and women that its growing total of population requires. It inhibits the usual corrective process by which the birthrate falls as standards rise. It sets up a vicious circle.

Nor can population statistics alone reveal the whole problem. The newer immigrants tend to be settled in new areas where there is space for housing and for farming; their presence also serves the general policy of 'creating facts' by extending economic control over sparsely peopled territory so as to buttress military command of it. This policy however not only increased their hardships but slowed the pace of integration by cutting them off physically from contact with acclimatized Israelis of the dominant cultural pattern, and from access to secondary education of the sort that could lead to higher studies.

All this roused more and more public concern and indeed alarm. After a few years of abortive attempts to mask the real position by such measures as lowering real standards to produce better apparent results, educational policy was radically changed so as to throw overboard myths about equality, face the facts as they were, and make realistic plans to correct them. The following summary account of the programmes that began to be introduced in 1962 is drawn from *Society, Schools and Progress in Israel,* by A. F. Kleinberger, who is the Associate Professor of Comparative Education in the Hebrew University.[1]

A Centre was set up for schools 'in need of special care', in distant areas or town slums, with 'culturally deprived' catchment areas, poor standards, ill-equipped teachers. By 1966–7 about a third of *all* Jewish primary schools were under the care of this Centre. Classes are smaller, books and equipment provided, teachers supported and guided by specialist visiting staffs. There are curricula and methods adapted to the needs respectively of children from deprived homes, the 'naturally' backward, and those with high ability handicapped by their background. Among the measures used are:

(1) Pre-school education in kindergartens for more three and four-year-olds, and the deliberate use of the compulsory 'fives' year to overcome handicaps. (This is to make up for the inability of many oriental families – illiterate mothers, non-Hebrew-speaking fathers – to induct their children into life in a modern Western society.)

(2) Showing mothers how to talk to their children so as to bring them on, and how to use toys and games.

(3) Extra-long working days for supplementary lessons in about a fifth of the schools.

(4) For some hundreds of classes, an extra-curricular month in summer, combining holiday-camp and class teaching.

(5) About 90 small remedial classes, usually for a year, for children specially backward in language, reading or arithmetic, and about 2,000 auxiliary study groups for slow learners.

(6) Text books and special teaching methods, based on research into the needs of children unused to the normal Western use of abstract ideas and symbols.

(7) Programmes of cultural broadening for poor-standard schools in outlying areas.

(8) Enrichment programmes for children in the top quarter of some primary classes, to help them on to secondary education and lessen the risk of drop-out among the able.

(9) A number of boarding schools for specially gifted children

from development towns and immigrant villages lacking in
normal openings for secondary education. Results here have
been strikingly good.

(10) A less expensive programme of 'day care' for children of the
same type and circumstance. This looks after about 10,000
'Afro-Asian' children; visiting tutors and extra summer
lessons take care of several thousands more.

This outline, which is not complete, is set out so as to make clear the
thoroughness and determination with which the most serious of the
social problems facing the Jewish community is being tackled. Professor
Kleinberger thinks it too early to look for results. He notes a very
sharp narrowing of the gap between the overall post-primary school
attendance rates of Western and Afro-Asian children, and a similar
relative improvement in the numbers enjoying the sort of academic
secondary education likeliest to lead on to universities. But he
scrupulously adds that it is impossible at present to know how much of
this improvement is due to education, how much to reduced poverty
and unemployment.

The programme, taken by itself, might be assessed as a bold and
intelligent response to a threatening national emergency, such as other
states also might have adopted, especially if they had compelling reasons
both for warding off domestic disruption and for making the most of
their human resources. That in itself is a debatable proposition, since
other states are not always so clear about their scale of values and the
action required to realize them. Nor are the established members of
other communities so ready for the social and personal adjustments
involved. But in fact the programme cannot be understood except in
a wide context. Let us be guilty of odious comparisons. America's colour
problem is a historical debt, not yet measurably under discharge.
Britain's owes something to a politico-moral idea, the idea of Commonwealth citizenship transcending national limits. But when the practical
consequences appeared the idea itself – though not the human obligations it had created – was soon jettisoned. Israel's education programme,
on the other hand, is one of the means to an end deliberately willed –
the end of making a national home for any and every Jew who needs
or wants one. Perhaps the various tasks and burdens this would involve
were not all specifically foreseen. But it is impossible to believe that the
people of Israel would have flinched or faltered at any prospect of
trouble ahead, whatever its form.

The world-wide problem of colour with its accompaniments of social, cultural and economic cleavage challenges men and nations to stand up and be counted in respect of their basic creeds, emotions and values. The extraordinary fact is that for the State of Israel the moral challenge, measured against its dimensions in other advanced countries, has hardly presented itself as such. There has been some prejudice, and it has thrown a little grit into the wheels of policy-making; but it has scarcely slowed, let alone stopped them. The unquestioning acceptance of the solidarity of the Jewish people, the faith that inspired the Law of Return, has triumphed. What the idea of our shared humanity has struggled, so far unsuccessfully, to achieve in the West, the shared identity of Jewry has achieved almost without a struggle. Whatever that identity may involve and imply, unmistakably it works.

Arabs

(i) 'WITHIN THY GATES'

What is our attitude towards the Arabs, who after all are our
partners in political as well as in social life whether we wish it
or no? What do we know about them or wish to know, that is
more than that which anti-Semites know of us? What have we
done to bring ourselves into more friendly relations with one
another, so that we might be one group, working at one task?

Aaron David Gordon asked these questions, long before the Jewish
State embodied political power and the responsibility it carries. Today
the questions remain. Now they relate to the 300,000 Arabs in pre-1967
Israel, a tenth of the population living mostly in Nazareth and perhaps
100 villages. They live peaceably. Under the test of the Six-Day War
they remained outwardly loyal, and took none of the endless opportunities for sabotage that offered themselves – not a bridge blown, not
a telephone wire cut. Their standard of life has risen, and not only
because of the effect of better technical methods. The old landowners
have gone; with them the old tenancy system – half the value of the
product paid in rent – and the old load of debt. The old well-to-do
middle and professional classes fled, and some of the sons of peasants
and workers are rising up to take their place as a new intelligentsia.
In a relatively classless community of peasants and workers, the rising
efficiency of agriculture frees a growing number to work at light
industries in the villages. Democratic municipal rule in the villages is
extending and the younger men play a growing part. Wages, working
conditions and public welfare are the same as for Jews: the Histadrut sees
to that, with a third of the Arab labour force enrolled among its
members. The Bedouin live more and more in permanent settlements.
Women play a greater part in productive work, and more girls get
some schooling: the female share of the primary school population rose

from less than a fifth when the State was founded to more than two fifths before the Six-Day War, and that in the teeth of traditional Muslim attitudes to women and their education.

If the spirit of Gordon walked into the Knesset today and asked his questions, the tally of answers would sound impressive. Indeed it is impressive, given the obstacles created by the sentimental ties between Arabs in Israel and the citizens of enemy states; the loss by flight in 1948 of most of the ablest and best educated; the poverty and degradation that were the starting point for many Arab communities; above all the dragging sheet-anchor of traditional ideas and practices. On the other hand positive attempts at social integration by the Histadrut and others have had limited success, and there is comparatively little industrial development. (Arabs provide most of the building labour.) Above all, the problem of educational backwardness, though not neglected, has evoked no such determined response, stirred no such spirit of urgency, as the cultural plight of the ingathered Afro-Asian Jews. Why not? The conditions are precisely similar in pattern, and of greater intensity. The shortage of teachers is more acute and their qualifications on the average lower. The number of children who get secondary education of any kind is pitifully small: in 1965–6 official statistics show that the percentage of Arabs at 'post-primary' schools was less than half that of Jews born in Asia and Africa and less than a third that of children of the same origin born in Israel. In 1961 (the latest figures available) the percentage of all Moslems who could not read or write was 62 (of females, 86) compared with 31 per cent and 44 per cent among Jews of Afro-Asian birth. These latter figures reflected the situation that evoked the special programme described earlier for Jews: the Arabs' still greater need evoked no such rescue operation. The peculiar difficulties of the latter case help to explain the difference in the two pictures as we see them: but they also underline the difference in response. It is surely safe to say that every reason put forward to explain the disparity between the educational status of the two ethnic groups would have been used as an argument for taking every conceivable step to narrow it – if the Arabs had been immigrant Jews.

Must not this outward appearance be evident to the Arab? And its inward meaning still more so? He could not fail to perceive that he is given second-class treatment because he is held to be a second-class citizen. He sees himself, too, as part of a defeated remnant, living among a dominant tribe which, tiny as it is, has three times worsted his own far more numerous people and shamed the glory of its military past.

He cannot fail to ask himself whether his conquerors do not also regard him as a second-class man. What answer do they allow him to give himself?

The whole domestic situation troubles some sensitive Jewish con- sciences and there are voluntary efforts to correct it. The thought may spread, to the point of a change in the policy of the State. The fact that it has not already done so is easy to understand, once one acknowledges one simple fact. Israel, which is in profession and in theory an egalita- rian social democracy, still retains in this vital respect – one that is little affected directly by problems of defence – the character of a sectarian state, with a ruling and a subordinate community, divided by their 'ethnic affiliation', to borrow the term from the national registration card. In this it falls short of the universalist teaching of Judaism, the thing that gives a measure of validity to its claims of Election and Mission. When will the lost vision of Aaron David Gordon be reborn?

(ii) THE GREAT DILEMMA

The Rabbi: Our relation to God is a closer one than if we had reached greatness already on earth.

The Ruler: This might be so, if your humility were voluntary; but it is involuntary, and if you had power you would slay.

The Rabbi: Thou hast touched our weak spot, O King of the Khazars. If the majority of us, as thou suggest, would learn humility towards God and his law from our low station, Providence would not have forced us to bear it for such a long period. Only the smallest portion thinks thus.

The Kuzari, 1140.

I should much rather see reasonable agreement with the Arabs on the basis of living together in peace than the creation of a Jewish State . . . my awareness of the essential nature of Judaism resists the idea of a Jewish State with borders, an army, and a measure of temporal power no matter how modest. I am afraid of the inner damage Judaism will sustain – especially from the development of a narrow nationalism within our own ranks, against which we have already had to fight strongly, even without a Jewish State. We are no longer the Jews of the Maccabee period. . . . If external necessity should after all compel us to assume this burden, let us bear it with tact and patience.

Albert Einstein, 1938.

Among Jewish labour circles any arrogance, brutality or provocativeness towards the neighbour has always been a thing of abhorrence. We did not come to this country as a 'superior race' . . . we came not in order to impose ourselves on others, but to liberate ourselves from the power others held over us.

Berl Katznelson (Zionist labour leader), 1940.

We have to cope with this complex aim of reaching general understanding and co-operation with the Arabs of the Middle East . . . it is up to the Arabs to understand that the UN Resolution can no longer be rescinded and that the Jews will not go beyond the boundaries fixed, or conquer any area outside them. This suspicion lurks in the hearts of many Arabs; it must be proved in every way possible that it is an unfounded suspicion.

Chaim Weizmann, *Trial and Error*, written in 1947.

The State of Israel . . . will devote itself to developing the Land for the good of all its inhabitants.

Proclamation of the State, 1948.

The State has been established in only a portion of the Land of Israel.

Government Year Book, 1951–2.

So long as I feel that I am defending my own home, the place where I live, I shall have the strength to do so. But the moment I feel that I am not defending my home or the very essence of my life, but something entirely different, it is clear that I shall not have the strength to educate my own sons to that. . . . It is to this that we should orient our education and on this we must stand firm.

Yishai the Soldier, 1967.

Judaea and Samaria.

Official Israeli titles of occupied Palestinian Arab territories, 1967.

It is a religious obligation not to return the newly occupied territories.

Sephardi Chief Rabbi, 1968 (in substance).

Extend the boundaries of our Land, just as Thou hast promised our forefathers, from the river Euphrates to the river of Egypt. Build your holy city, Jerusalem, capital of Israel; and there may your temple be established as in the days of Solomon.

Prayer for Independence Day issued by the Religious Kibbutz Movement, 1968.

I do not want to be shot at by people who have a just cause, who have no alternative. I think everything possible must be done so that people convinced of the justice of their action should not shoot at us. We are strong because we are in the right, but we have to convince ourselves anew every time. We must not take it for granted a priori that we are always and at all times, whatever we do, in the right.

Kibbutz mother, Shdemot, 1968.

I am duty-bound to re-examine my own motives in order to confirm that what might have appeared to me to be essential for the preservation of my existence is not in fact a camouflage for the power-drive within me. Only through a continual and relentless struggle with myself can there be any assurance that this injustice I commit, as an individual or a community, is indeed no more than the absolute minimum.

Aryeh Simon, Youth-Village Director, 1969.

We must ask ourselves whether the price of armed security might be too high, if we have to pay for it with the loss of other values which have marked Jewish character throughout the ages.

Rabbi J. J. Cohen, Head of Hillel House, 1970.

It is my position (and I am sure that this is also the fundamental position of the majority of the Jewish people in this land) that there is only one nation to whom the land belongs in trust and by covenant promise, and that is the Jewish people. No temporary demographic changes can alter this basic fact which is the bedrock of the Jewish faith; just as one wife does not have two husbands so one land does not have two sovereign nations in possession of it. You will understand that the covenant analogy is what links these two terms together.

Dr Harold Fisch, Rector of Bar-Ilan University, 1970.

The only people in Israel who doubt the practical wisdom, and essential rightness, of standing on the existing military boundaries until a secure peace is signed are small groups of the ultra-orthodox on the right and even smaller numbers of the 'new left'. The rest believe that the threat of extermination still hangs over them, as it did over German Jewry in the days of the Nazis, and that the record of past promises by other powers gives them no encouragement to rely on anything short of firm international guarantees and a pledged Arab commitment. Nor do they think that even this amounts to more than the best approximation they can hope for to absolute security.

The differences among them are not about this strategic objective but about the tactical means of achieving it and the terms of settlement. It is here that the different attitudes towards religion show themselves. The Greater Israel Movement includes both hard-line secular 'chauvinists' who see the interest of the State as such groups normally do, and those for whom the claims of religion mean insistence on the ancient limits of the Land. On the other hand, there is a body of intellectuals dedicated to upholding the ethical standards of Judaism in the conduct of the State towards Arab fellow-citizens within and Arab states without. For them the interest of Israel is not confined to survival: it requires that survival must be on a basis of justice, mercy and a certain humility in deciding where the ultimate truth of the situation may lie. They protest, sometimes actively, against the use of tough measures. They are more sensitive to the risks of the existing situation, military as well as moral, and would take more risks of an opposite kind, believing in the possibility of reducing the intensity of Arab hostility and mistrust by showing that they are unjustified. To 'win over another man' can be read with or without a comma after 'win'; one can gain a point or gain a friend. This movement would aim at the second.

Between these two the general body of public opinion would probably disavow both extremes. Support for the Greater Israel Movement is not widespread. Not many would go as far as the opposite group, but sympathy with its ideas tends to grow. Some react to Arab intransigence as the average citizen of any civilized country would in like circumstances; others are more troubled at the prospect of an indefinite siege and its effects on the basic values of the community. Among this number are some of the most thoughtful and a few of the most influential of the younger men on Kibbutzim and in the towns.

It is outside our purpose to assess the specific tactical issues that constantly face the Government, or to suggest guidelines for a settlement. These are not questions for outsiders, whose skins are not at risk and whose own countries' records give them more title to be preached at than to preach. What is significant for our purpose is the appearance in this most urgent and critical arena of the same tension between the 'particularist' and the 'universalist' sides of the Jewish tradition as we have seen in other contexts. It is a tension felt in every free country which sees the threat of the times and must try to do justice to its own interests and the wider need. In Israel the two-way pull is stronger. Not only are the dangers greater and more immediate, but the entire ideological background of the State gives a keener edge to every moral dilemma. The Jewish tradition lays more emphasis on communal ethics than does the individualist tradition of the West.

If and when negotiations take place and reach their climax, the tension and the dilemma will move from words to deeds and from discussion to choice. Boundary questions will intertwine ideology with expediency. It might be judged worth while to give up a good deal for a secure and recognized base, even if constricted, as the Jewish community was ready to do with the UN partition plan in 1947. But Jerusalem – 'Zion incarnate as a holy hill' – raises deeper issues. Here is where the universal idea and the claim to particular possession meet and, it would seem, confront. What is it about the holy city that the Jewish people feel that they cannot outwardly share to the full? What does it stand for, that they alone must retain the right to defend? Is there some essential that, by sharing, they would lose? Would they sacrifice that essential, if they shared it? Does its retention as their very own further their universal mission or obstruct it?

These are the questions they must in due time answer, and much may hang, for us all, on what they say.

Diaspora

The purpose of this chapter is to describe the relation between Israel and the Diaspora, or rather two Diaspora countries, chosen as examples because in their different ways they are most closely involved with her affairs. They exhibit, perhaps better than any others, those features of the relationship which have most significance for the State, and the dispersed communities as a whole.

Nearly four out of five of the fourteen million Jews in the world live in three countries: the United States, Russia and Israel. One of the five, being Russian, is forced to live apart. Another one (slightly less in fact) is Israeli. Two are American. When wealth is reckoned as well as numbers the American Jewish community emerges as predominant in the Diaspora, and by a wide margin. It exerts considerable though not decisive influence on American external policy, and Israel's relations with the USA are of a significance that dwarfs those with any other country. Everyone in Israel is well aware of it. The Jewish community in Britain, reckoned by the latest estimates to number about 410,000, is the third largest in the 'lesser' bracket, after France and the Argentine. It is a 300 year settlement, the only one in Europe not disrupted in that period. Cecil Roth remarked of it in 1964 that 'of the more or less healthy Jewries of the Old World – indeed, of the world generally – we are now among the most venerable if not indeed . . . the most venerable of all.' It is part of a country which even in its diminished state has something of a world-wide position in politics, military affairs, trade, finance and communications. As the mandatory power, Britain left a well-marked imprint on Israeli life, from the fabric of the Common Law to the language of the sign-posts and street name-boards. Its imperial record had some very dark spots, but most Israelis now remember without rancour. Many of the older among them fought the Nazis in British uniforms and in spite of later events remember the fact with some pride. There is evidence that the British people – not their governments – rank with Americans at the top of the popularity league among Israeli schoolchildren, a fact which any British visitor who knows a little history must be slightly abashed to learn. It may owe something to Ben-Gurion's occasional use of the story of Britain in 1940 to point the moral of what a small country, alone and with its back to the wall, could do. Whatever the causes, as part of the Diaspora scene Britain looms up second, a little larger than life. This top-bracketing owes much to the virtual disappearance of the mother-communities of the bulk of Israel's population, in Russia, Poland, Hungary, Germany and the Arab Afro-Asian countries.

For some of the purposes of this chapter, the Jewish communities of the two countries – quaintly lumped together in Israel in the classical Hebrew term 'Anglo-Saxonim' – can be considered together. Both enjoy full political liberties, have on the whole done well, and suffer some social disabilities (much more serious in the USA). Both have a majority of Jews who – by all report – combine some outward con-formity and an attachment to the Jewish community and Jewish 'cultural values', with a lack of real personal commitment to any positive religious faith. Both these conformist majorities are a little uneasy about the meaning of their Jewish identity; both responded emotionally and financially to Israel's trials and triumphs of 1967; both continue to show this increased concern for, and (up to a point) commitment to, that country. The whole picture and every element in it should be painted in stronger colours for America. That country is outstandingly the biggest source of funds for the programmes of the Jewish Agency, which has outgrown its British parentage and early nursing. At this point of generalization it will be more convenient to separate the two particular roads.

Let us begin with the most marked difference in their structures. In America orthodox Jews, measured by synagogue affiliation, are less than a third of the total, with Conservative and Reform Judaism sharing the balance. In Britain these dissident groups – called respectively, and confusingly, Reform and Liberal – number between them about a tenth of the total, a fact which their comparative social prominence and London concentration tend to conceal.

In Britain, on the evidence of Jewish witnesses, the community is less and less marked out by religious observance. The rate of inter-marriage, with the great majority of the children lost to the Jewish community, is estimated variously from 15–25 per cent. The latter figure was mentioned in a survey carried out by the *Jewish Chronicle*, the premier organ of Jewry, in 1969; it was one of the facts that led the paper to conclude that the ties between Jews and Judaism are getting weaker. Figures of another kind point the same way. Marriages in synagogue, one of the surest marks of some sort of conformity, have fallen steadily in number. In the British community as a whole, the ratio of people married in church to the number of deaths is 127 : 100. Among the Jewish population the ratio is 72 : 100. Field surveys suggest that 60 per cent of Jewish students do not think of religion as an essential part of their Jewishness. But the majority are very conscious of Israel: this tie, and realization of the meaning of the holocaust, are the two principal ingredients in their sense of their Jewish identity. About 20 per cent feel entirely dissociated from Jewish life whether in Israel or the Diaspora, while the same proportion are loyal to traditional Judaism. It may be more than a coincidence that these exact proportions have also been found in Israel for the completely alienated and the totally committed, respectively.

The extent and quality of Jewish education in Britain have been heavily criticized from within the community. It would seem that various forms of part-time education fail to convey more than a smattering of Jewish knowledge and almost no Hebrew, with the result that 'about half of the growing Jewish generation will be unable to take any active part in Jewish religious life, and it is difficult to see how this half . . . can be retained as an integral part of our community'.[1] Again, 'the number of teachers who combine adequate Jewish knowledge with sound pedagogical training is nil'.[2] Two American rabbis, experts on Jewish education, were quoted in the *American Jewish Year Book* (1969) as having reported, after a special investigation, that many of the problems of Jewish education in Britain were 'insurmountable' except by attendance at Jewish day schools. The number of these has been increasing, but only 11,000 Jewish children out of 60,000 attend them, and the fraction which goes on to a secondary education with a Jewish background is very much smaller still. It must always be a question how far a purely elementary education can equip a child to stand up to the incessant, powerful pressures of the dominant secular culture.

In a careful, detailed survey, *Leeds Jewry*,[3] the author Ernest Krausz drew in 1963 some conclusions which probably applied reasonably well to most other urban communities. He saw the main cohesive links of Jewry in Leeds as its own social exclusiveness, matched by that of the host community, together with the weakened but still persisting influence of religion. He saw no reason to count on the continuance of the former – the latter, religion, would last longer.

Superficially, this looks like the picture of a community seriously threatened by shrinkage and decline, its religious adherence a shell increasingly hollowed out by the power of the environment, leaving nothing durable. To the doctrinaire Zionist, it is the proof of his contention that a national culture must be linked to a national home, and that (as one such wrote) 'the only living parts of Jewish cultural life [in England] are those directly or indirectly connected with the complete national existence of Israel'.[4] There are however some points that tell the other way. One is the proven durability of the 'remnant' of strictly orthodox, fundamentalist Judaism. As one speaker said at the 1964 Conference, referred to in notes 1 and 2, the extreme right-wing groups 'guarantee the future of the community better than the most expensive synagogues'. A second is the possible renascence of Jewish religious vitality, in more contemporary forms; of this, some Jews believe signs are already visible. The third is the fact of Israel, especially since the galvanic shock administered by its victory in 1967. This is a new factor of Jewish consciousness and cohesion. It is already clear that there is strong feeling for Israel, taking form in an eagerness to help morally and materially: it is also clear that this stops short of the will to emigrate except for a trickle. What else may be involved is a question to which we will return.

The picture in the United States is in two crucial respects similar to the British. The mixed-marriage rate is estimated at from 17–20 per cent, and the position of Jewish education is a cause of deep concern. As to the latter, the gist of many lamentations is summed up, and factually documented, in a striking survey by Walter Ackerman.[5] Despite a manifold increase in the number of Jewish day schools, now 7,300 in all, less than a seventh of Jewish children is reported to attend them. A battery of fact and argument, with some rhetoric, is deployed to show that no part-time school, of whatever Jewish denomination, can achieve what is declared to be the broad purpose of the Jewish school – 'to contribute to the continued existence of the Jews as an identifiable group.' Of those who attend Jewish day schools at the junior level, a very small proportion acquire secondary or high school education in the same religious milieu. An even more radical weakness is the 'desperate' shortage of teachers. 'The American Jewish community has never been able to produce a sufficient number of native-born teachers.' The full requirement is for 2,000 teachers: the number graduating each year is about 200, of whom 125 actually teach, a significant fraction of these being Israelis. Jewish education is in one powerful particular flying in the face of normal American values: it 'serves no pragmatic ends', and offers no marketable skills (except presumably in the Jewish teaching profession, where a vigorous sellers' market ought to exist). One recalls Rabbi Kook calling for an education 'against the stream of time': not the most hopeful enterprise in contemporary America. Professor Moshe Davis, a Professor of American origin, Director of the Institute of Contemporary Jewry in the Hebrew University, Jerusalem, and a recent student of his native country, wrote in 1969 of 'the spreading eclipse of Judaism'; he reported that he found 'the roots of Jewish culture in the U.S. . . . withering away', and its position relative to the dominant American culture growing steadily weaker. He concludes that the threat is not the vanishing Jew but vanishing Judaism. Similarly Nathan Rotenstreich (Rector of the Hebrew University, 1965–9) wrote of America that 'Euthanasia is the Jewish question'.

Up to this point the American picture is remarkably like the British. There are also the same countervailing possibilities, to lighten the gloom. There are the obstinately entrenched fundamentalists, and the hope of a revivified Judaism in some less rigid form. There is also Israel. But here the picture becomes a good deal more complex.

Israel, as promise and then as presence, has long been a considerable factor in American Jewish thought. Zionism, like synagogue membership, has been a respectable Jewish posture, and a screen to cover retreat from any profound religious commitment. The Six-Day War was the occasion of a tremendous upsurge of emotional loyalty, concern and commitment. This was not just a flash-in-the-pan: strong and widely based financial support has continued, and emigration to Israel though still very slight has grown noticeably, most of it apparently by Jews with religious attachment. Tourist visits to Israel have greatly increased, as have more systematic cultural and educational exchanges. The question is whether all this makes of the State that new inspirational force which the condition of Judaism in the USA appears to call for, and troubled observers like Professor Davis are anxious to see. There are three question marks. One is raised by some sociological data which is not reassuring.

Early in 1969 a postal inquiry was conducted among rabbis and synagogue presidents of the three major Jewish denominations: Orthodox, Conservative and Reform. The main purpose was to discover the degree of their attachment to Israel. The questions were whether Jewish life in America should have an American or an Israeli cultural centre, whether Israel should be the spiritual centre of world Jewry, whether support for it was a religious obligation for American Jews, and whether Jews should move to Israel. The results are described in an article by Charles Liebman of Bar-Ilan University, 'The Role of Israel in the Ideology of American Jewry'.[6] In his own words:

> Orthodox are far more identified with Israel than are the non-orthodox. This is true of . . . rabbis . . . synagogue presidents . . . leaders of a secular Jewish organisation. . . . Secondly . . . Israel plays a greater role in the ideology of rabbis than of laymen. . . . Finally, and perhaps of greatest importance, the data suggest that with the exception of Orthodox rabbis, Israel does not really play a central role in the Jewish ideology of any group. Certainly, among a sample of leaders from secular and religious organisations, Israel does not play the kind of Jewish role which its spokesmen and friends envisage for it. To this, we need only add the obvious; that the Jewish consciousness and Jewish ideology in which Israel plays a small part is itself only a small part of the self-identity and total ideology of the American Jew.

The second query about Israel's world leadership and its acceptance in America is raised by the phenomenon of the New Left. This product of the alienation of a section of the rising generation in America – of course including those perennial rebels the Jews – is apt to puzzle the cultural establishment in Israel even more than in America. To find some Jews supporting al-Fatah is a far greater shock even than the preference of exiled Algerian Jews for France over Israel. Yet the explanation is plain when the facts are regarded together. The Arab is seen as the underdog; he is allotted to the third world; his poverty and backwardness are claims on universalist sympathies. Israel on the other hand looks undemocratic in its treatment of its own Arabs, and harshly militarist in its occupation of others' territories and in its security measures. Its confrontation with the guerrillas calls up the ghost of American forces dealing with guerrillas in Vietnam. Moreover Israel is the darling of the American (Jewish) establishment, with whom one's Zionist parents are naturally and scornfully identified. Its social-democratic ideology in so far as it is realized or understood carries little appeal to American middle-class young people – the New

Left is not, on the whole, a movement of the under-privileged. In a word some young Jews like assertive nationalism in Israel little better than anywhere else. They do not perceive its idealistic content, and find it a distasteful ingredient in the mixture of ethnic, cultural and religious values that is offered them by Israel, or on its behalf, as their own proper portion in the world. Their dislike of the nationalism of the Jewish State and disbelief in its universalist aspects are, while they last, obstacles to any realization of the vision of the 'centrality of Israel' as light and saviour of American Jewry. While they last: whether the New Left is a phase that will pass or, as some believe, the first sign of an impending break with the pervasive conservatism of American thought, is a question outside our present scope.

The third element of doubt concerns the situation of the entire American Jewish community in its non-Jewish environment. To envisage a recurrence of anti-Semitism as a serious force anywhere in the free world might seem far-fetched. It has many times seemed so in the past two centuries, during the phases of apparent tranquillity before it reappeared. Few of the German Jews living their comfortable twentieth-century lives found Nazi extremism credible until it was upon them. Indeed it would be possible without much distortion to present the history of Jewry since the Enlightenment as a series of ideological splits and divisions, each checked or suppressed by the external compulsion of an outburst somewhere in the world of the ancient rage. The history of anti-Semitism shows that it has assumed an almost infinite variety of forms, from as many mutually contradictory superficial causes. On past precedent, any situation of economic disturbance, social unrest or spiritual malaise could give rise to it. In America certain early signs have been described, in the magazine *Interplay*, by a British journalist of some distinction, Henry Fairlie.[7] He finds that the young dismiss his warnings as atrocity stories outdated by thirty years, but he sees as one of the chief dangers precisely the conjunction of anti-Jewish prejudice among the 'old right' with the 'respectable' idealism of the New Left, including its anti-Jewish ingredient. Thus in America, Israel and local Jewry could find themselves bracketed together as targets for non-Jewish prejudice. This is clearly a complex and confusing situation for the young Jews who share the anti-Israel position. They may have to make a choice. Into this pattern the phenomenon of black anti-Semitism also fits comprehensibly. Jews, who appear slightly off-white to gentile anti-Semites, are identified by 'black power' with the white oppressors. They are not only oppressors in their own right, as landlords or prosperous shop-keepers, but are also a minority who might have been expected to help oppressed blacks and did not. This too brings Israel into the picture not only as an oppressor State, but as a beneficiary of Zionist money made by exploiting blacks.

It is not necessary to argue from this confusion of ideas and emotions that serious anti-Semitism in America is likely. The mere possibility is enough. The effect it may have in bringing buried fears nearer the surface of Jewish minds and so checking communal disintegration is from one point of view a sort of advantage. But there is a disturbing element in the situation which should be remembered by those both in Israel and the Diaspora who plead or work for a greater outward identification with Israel on the part of Jews abroad. It is not absolutely certain that the link with Israel would always strengthen the situation of the American community. In any country in turmoil a constituent group which repeatedly asserted an extra-territorial link with another sovereign state might be inviting trouble. The 'Israel lobby' in America (the question is much less acute in Britain) has enjoyed a good deal of friendly indulgence from public opinion. This could begin to change if the policies of Israel diverged from the interests of America as seen by any large section of opinion there, or if the claim to a sort of dual nationality – at least to a nationality and a half – were too asser-tively pressed by the local Jewish community. This warning has in fact been issued by some Zionist leaders. There are however other voices, less politically aware, who press their hopes of Jewish trans-national identification without much apparent realization of the problems it might bring. Here, in fact, is a quite new form of our familiar dilemma. On the one hand, if the link between American Jewry and Israel is mainly sentimental, involving only a common history, some tradition, and the 'universalist' aspects of Judaism which are (in theory) common ground between the two countries, then what becomes in the long run of the Zionist view of Israel and the special Zionist theses? But if the tie rests largely on the sense of shared destiny, or the common membership of a 'community of fate', or the vision of Judaism as an indissoluble union of religion and nationality, the position of dispersed communities which retain a strong Jewish identity might become dangerously exposed.

To assess this dilemma one needs to remind oneself of the attitudes found in Israel towards the Diaspora. Orthodox and near-Orthodox Israelis are not, as such, at the centre of this question. It is the nationalist-

Zionist element in the ideology of the State, especially among the younger citizens, which is here more influential and relevant. To most of these younger people Israel has been the natural goal of all Jewish aspiration: its centrality was axiomatic. For some time after the foundation of the State it seemed to many indoctrinated young nationalists that the Diaspora must be inhabited by half-men, or at least half-Jews, an inferior breed who rejected not only Jewish values but socialist ones too. Until the early '50s, perhaps later, the Communist countries had a distinct ideological attraction, most powerful with the most left-wing segment but extending beyond it. (The need to take sides in the Korean war was one of the issues that split the Kibbutz movements.) The Six-Day War brought to a head a radical shift of attitudes of which earlier signs had appeared. The Russians by ranging themselves firmly on the wrong side removed the last shreds of sympathy with Soviet ideology, now finally revealed as a sham. The stay-at-home capitalists of the West turned out to be the State's only friends. The solidarity of Jewry was a good deal more than a myth fathered by Zionist oratory. It had power even if it did not issue in Aliya. The Diaspora's existence and well-being were things a Sabra could value and cherish in his own interest. But besides that, the recent menace to Israel gave him a new sympathy with Jews abroad. He could see them for the first time as living like himself under the threat of nameless evil, with parents who had perhaps suffered the ultimate penalty, and without even the Israeli army to protect them. It brought home to him that there might be other sorts of courage than the military virtues. The 'community of fate' became more of a reality.

In the years since the war the meaning of the relationship has been more carefully considered. How should Israelis weigh the claims of Israel on the Diaspora against the claims of the dispersed communities on Israel? What could they reasonably look for, what provide? Should they make an issue of increased Aliya and challenge the communities abroad to produce it, or content themselves with fostering general support? Should they hold themselves out as an answer to the problems of Jewish identity abroad? Or confine themselves to keeping alive the sense of common identity and concern and see what comes of it? In view of the problems raised by the New Left in America and their repercussions in Israel itself, what kind of common identity is there and how far to be counted on? All these questions are being asked and discussed, publicly and privately, in Israel.

What seems to be happening is a divergence between traditional theory and current practice. Zionist ideology still points to life in Israel as the true and proper aim of the Jews in the Diaspora, but a certain realism can be detected between the lines. As Dr E. Schweid wrote in a Zionist publication: 'Even if you know that not every Jew will immigrate to Israel you must say as an educator that the fulfilment of Judaism entails *aliyah* . . . *aliyah* is a Jewish ideal that immigrants fulfil.' The two elements in world Jewry are in fact beginning to take one another for granted and to devote increasing thought and effort to the practical work of helping to solve one another's problems. As a prime example, the parlous state of Jewish education in Britain, America and some other Western countries is to be remedied in some degree by the programmes of teacher training conducted not only in the colleges in Israel maintained for the purpose by the Zionist authorities but by the Hebrew University's 'Centre for Jewish Education in the Diaspora' inaugurated in 1968. Its scope includes the training of teachers, supervisors and administrators, research into the problems of Diaspora education, the development of curricula and materials for class teaching, and the organization and training of working teachers in Israel who wish to teach abroad for a time. The degrees offered are B.A., M.A. and PhD.; the University's standards and the respect in which its degrees are held should mean that these courses will play a significant part in mitigating a serious weakness in the life of Jewish communities abroad. The number of students taking degree courses is over a hundred in all. This is a down-to-earth demonstration of the 'centrality of Israel' in the life of Jews abroad. It denotes an acceptance by the Israeli nation of an obligation to strengthen the Diaspora, and an acknowledgment of its active interest in so doing.

Israel's own needs for people, for help in absorbing them, and for the money required for these and other tasks have been met in good measure by the World Zionist Organisation, by the Jewish Agency acting as its executive arm in Israel, and by a number of fund-raising bodies abroad, outside the Zionist Organisation but containing a number of prominent Zionists among their leaders. In 1970 a significant reorganization of these bodies was agreed upon, to take effect in 1971. It seems likely to focus more attention on getting urgent things done, and perhaps rather less on abstract discussions about high policy. The interest and importance of these may lessen as the State and its partners abroad settle down to the ideological *status quo* and grapple with the difficult practical problems facing them all. The effect of the changes is to separate the Agency from the Zionist

Organisation, place it under a governing authority on which the 'outside' fund-raising bodies share representation equally with that organization, and give to each of the two its own defined province of work. The enlarged Agency will be responsible for help with higher education and with the absorption of immigrants by support of agricultural settlements and health and welfare services. This brings the wealth of business experience embodied in the newly incorporated fund-raising bodies to bear on a range of practical problems of major importance to the prosperity of the State. It should enable them to mobilize technical manpower and expertise from abroad, and it makes the whole enterprise resemble a vast technical aid and assistance programme, funded by those in charge of it, and drawing upon a massive reserve of devoted loyalty. Alongside this and complementary to it, are the organized efforts of the powerful Jewish business leadership, especially in America and Britain, to build up industrial investment and introduce new productive and distributive knowhow into the 'private sector' of Israel's economy.

The World Zionist Organisation is to retain its responsibilities for the Jewish National Fund and for existing youth, cultural and information functions. Above all it will continue to be responsible in the Diaspora for immigration into Israel. This appears to mean that, with its hands free of the duties it is handing over to the enlarged Agency, it will have a better chance to demonstrate by results the continuing vitality of the original Zionist idea. There are still those in Israel (and some abroad) who maintain that Zionism stands or falls by the practical witness of Aliya. Circumstances since the Six-Day War are favourable for success in that test, if the standards of success are realistically set. The total of immigrants expected in 1970-1 is 45,000, including a good fraction of well-qualified men and women from America and Britain. It would be a tiny proportion of the Jews in those countries but a useful tally for Israel. It is likely that the attention of Israelis will focus more on those who do come and less on the vaster numbers who do not, regarding these latter not as renegades but as worthy partners, if not quite worth their weight in gold, at least a substantial hard-currency asset.

The entire relationship is a familiar one in Jewish history but unique in today's world scene. The political scientist may find some interest in the fact that the most profoundly rooted of all nationalisms should be the one to pose the sharpest theoretical challenge to the concept itself. (The Jewish traditionalist will not find it unexpected.)

There are strains and stresses, actual and potential, affecting all parties concerned – the State, the dispersed communities and their host countries. Two of the main ones have been noted: on one hand the question of dual allegiance, on the other the problems presented for non-orthodox communities in America by the attitudes of some of their more extreme fellow-citizens in combination with that of the rabbinical authorities in Jerusalem.

It is not to be expected that the Diaspora communities, who have to contend with their own kinds of conflict between religious and secular Jewish opinions, could be exempt from the effect of these in their special, and specially significant, Israeli forms. If Israel is to be a spiritual and cultural centre for world Jewry, its own mixed ideologies may give the relationship a peculiar character. Orthodox Jews in Britain, and no doubt in America too, may look a little askance at an influx of Israeli teachers of uncertain purity of doctrine, and may wonder what their own fellow-citizens will bring back from teacher-training courses in a largely secular university however distinguished its standards of scholarship. Indeed the political aspect of the Israel-Diaspora relationship presents by no means its only paradox. The idea of a secular State and a predominantly secular community as the spiritual centre of the Jewish people raises complex questions. Of course the idea of an extra-territorial focus of faith and religious teaching is not itself unique – the Roman Catholic Church and some of its great Orders present parallels. What marks out the Jewish case is the identity of faith and nationhood, as the historic taproot from which the political world-centre has grown. In the province of this chapter, like the others, the question-mark is inescapable.

What is a Jew?

Jewish Identity: Descriptive

'Historical Judaism is not merely a religion, like Christianity or
Islam. Judaism is a body of culture. Unique historical conditions
which brought the life of the Jewish nation under the dominance
of religion converted Judaism into an all-embracing world view
which encompasses religious, ethical, social, messianic, political and
philosophical elements. In each of these areas history has piled up
layer upon layer. The Bible, the Talmud, Rabbinical Judaism,
rationalist Jewish theology, Jewish mysticism are not merely
chapters in Jewish religious teaching but also stages in the development of Judaism. Judaism is broad enough and variegated enough
so that any man in Israel can draw from its source according to
his spirit and outlook. The orthodox Jew accepts all the principles
of religious faith and practice formed in the course of generations
and rigidly set down in the codes of law and in the ordinances of
the rabbis. The 'reformed' Jew rejects the decisions of the rabbis
and even the laws of the Talmud and accepts only the religious
principles, laws and obligations of the Bible. Adherents of
rationalist theology find satisfaction in the religious theology of
the middle ages. The free-thinking Jew who accepts only ethical
teaching can find an exalted social and moral world view in the
teachings of the Hebrew Prophets. The ethical teachings of the
Prophets can well become 'the religion of the future', the moral
doctrine of a free society. All those who base their religion on
poetic content will find in the Bible and in the mediaeval Jewish
literature a source of poetry that fills the soul with magic
splendour. Followers of mysticism will find a great treasure house
in the Kabbala and to a greater degree in Hasidism, the 'religion
of the heart'. Thus one may be a Jew according to the teaching
of the Prophets or the Talmud, according to Moses Maimonides
or the *Shulhan Arukh*,[1] according to Moses Mendelssohn or the

Besht,[2] according to Geiger[3] or Samson Raphael Hirsch,[4] as long as one does not reject entirely the national idea, which is not a matter of theory but a historical fact.'[5]

Dubnow's impressive disquisition would appear to exhaust all the possibilities. What it does is to beg the fundamental question. In its simplest terms the question is whether Judaism makes Jews, or Jews make Judaism: whether the religion is a spiritual force that has shaped the Jewish people or is merely the sum and substance of what that people thinks and does. Dubnow's third sentence contains the ambiguity and almost conceals it.

In *Judaism: a Portrait*,[6] Leon Roth writes:

Judaism is not to be considered in terms of the Jews but the Jews in terms of Judaism. Judaism is not what some or all Jews happen as a fact to do. It is what Jews should be doing (but often are not doing) as members of a holy people. Judaism comes first. It is not a product but a programme and the Jews are the instruments of its fulfilment.

That short manifesto can do duty not only for the orthodox of all shades but for every Jew who puts his religion first and has his reason for doing so. There may be legitimate differences about the content of the 'programme' (the strictly orthodox would deny that): there can be none about its primacy.

Once it is maintained that the programme is a human achievement or, inherently, a human ideal, something that emerges from human effort or must be described in terms of it, the ground changes completely. When Ahad Ha'am, speaking for a myriad 'seculars', Zionist and other, describes Judaism as neither religion nor any other of the 'forms of culture' but as 'the national creative power' which can express itself in both or either, he is turning Roth's 'instrument' into the prime mover, making Judaism the weapon forged by Jewry's native genius to ensure its survival.

Neither of these two positions has any difficulty in 'explaining' the other in its own terms, or achieving an intellectual reconciliation on the basis of its own supremacy. To the religious Jew his secular colleague, in so far as he is more than an unthinking pagan, is one who enjoys the divine legacy without acknowledging the testator, who accepts the uniqueness of the Jewish people as an ultimate fact, with no attempt to understand its cause or condition. To him, this is a dangerous distortion, which leaves the identity of the Jewish people without solid foundation, open to the destructive power of time and chance. His own faith in God and in the mission of Israel assures him that all cannot finally be lost, but if Jewish disloyalty to that mission goes far enough and extends widely enough he must expect another falling away of the majority, another exile of some sort, another purification by suffering. Meanwhile he continues his own witness, by faithful performance of his duty to God and his fellowman: a duty that comprises both moral and ritual observance.

The thoughtful secular Jew, committed to his non-religious philosophy, regards the religion of Judaism as something that has survived its usefulness. Its great contribution has been the code of individual and social morality which has civilized the Western World and is now embodied in its thought and life. The ritual aspect, once perhaps a means to solidarity and survival, is now an offence against modern man's reason and the evolutionary, scientific code by which he lives: a dangerous obstacle, also, to the acceptance by the younger generation of what is good and true in the moral teaching, and a divisive threat to the unity of the community. The intrusion of rabbinical authority into the most intimate province of personal life is something which, according to his temperament, he will resist and evade, or endure in the name of the unity of the Jewish people or – perhaps – of the Jewish State.

Between these two is a graded spectrum of belief, embracing probably a little more than half the population of Israel, which ranges from a near acceptance of the orthodox position, given a little flexibility or laxity, to a position distinguished from the secular only by a few residual traces of observance – a rare, possibly annual, visit to the synagogue and the retention of the Bar-Mitzvah ceremony for the sons. To the religious believer, this spectrum of belief is also the downward path to assimilation – a process not confined to the Diaspora (where it ends in full absorption into the non-Jewish community) but signifying in Israel absorption into the prevailing atmosphere of the modern world: by stages materialist, permissive, decadent. The validity of religious observance lies in its being a divine command: but the believer finds the proof of the validity in what he regards as the observable fact that any departure from it is not viable. Once the absolute truth of revealed Law is questioned, once its strictness is abandoned, the door is open to every aberration: aberrations inevitably must and historically do follow. It is a position that has often been argued on behalf of many kinds of religious orthodoxy. Bernard

Shaw understood the strength of the argument. In *St. Joan* he used it twice, first in the mouth of the Bishop of Beauvais, denouncing the right of private judgment on spiritual matters:

> What will the world be like when The Church's accumulated wisdom and knowledge and experience, its councils of learned, venerable, pious men, are thrust into the kennel by every ignorant labourer or dairymaid whom the devil can puff up with the monstrous self-conceit of being directly inspired from heaven?

Then the Inquisitor:

> Heresy at first seems innocent and even laudable; but it ends in ... a monstrous horror of unnatural wickedness ... these diabolical madnesses ... begin always by vain and ignorant persons setting up their own judgment against the Church, and taking it upon themselves to be the interpreters of God's will.

The language is extreme, though not more so than that of Neturei Karta; the logic is the same. So, in Jewish experience, is history's evidence of the practical consequences – 'fallings away, vanishings.'

In theory, nothing could be wider than the rift between the adherent of strictly orthodox Judaism and the Jew whose conformity is limited and superficial or the committed secular humanist. The world views are opposed – a God-centred or a man-centred universe. The scales of values are reversed in principle and widely different in practice. The same of course might be said of corresponding differences in any advanced Western state: but the underlying circumstances make the division in Israel sharper. In other advanced nations the religious differences for which men used to kill one another have lost their tension and their central position.[7] In Europe the disrupted solidarity which bred the wars of religion ended three or four centuries ago, and *de facto* national solidarities have grown again in looser, more comprehensive, less ideological forms. It is not much over a century since the solidarity of the ghetto was seriously disrupted: the edges are still jagged and the divided partners are both part of the fabric of the State. Something too must be allowed for the fierce intensity of Jewish life and of Jewish belief: whether one puts it down to Genesis or to genes it makes for strenuous living and little outward tolerance. The disruption is even reflected in the educational process by which a community keeps its continuity and patterns its own future. We have seen how radical the classroom division is.

What then is it that holds the community together? The first, common-sense reply is that we cannot be sure because the Jewish community has not yet had the opportunity to be itself. For two thousand years – arguably, for longer – the Jewish people has existed 'over against': over against the surrounding Roman or pagan or Muslim or Christian world which surrounded it. Now, the State of Israel exists, as it has done from its inception, over against the Arabs and, in a less military sense, over against the world. In its corporate form it has inherited the millennial role of the individual Jew: to be different, to be apart, to be pressed upon by enemies or, at best, by friends who say 'you may be able to live at peace but it must be on our terms', to be burdened interminably by self-consciousness. One is tempted to define Jewish identity as simply the mark of the man who never stops vexing himself about what is Jewish identity. There is a French tag (probably misremembered): *Je suis Cassandre, mise à la terre pour dire aux hommes que je suis Cassandre, mise à la terre pour dire aux hommes que....* There is also a Hasidic saying which is in point. It is attributed to Rabbi Mendel of Kotzk. 'If I am I, simply because I am I, and thou art thou, simply because thou art thou; then I am I and thou art thou. But if I am I because thou art thou, and thou art thou because I am I, then I am not I and thou art not thou.' There was a film not long ago in which a Jewish character said in effect that what made a Jew was other people's thinking him a Jew. In Tel Aviv and Jerusalem the Israeli audiences laughed loudly at the line: a palpable hit. Perhaps they did not laugh so loud in Westchester or St. John's Wood.

While the barriers remain the world can never be sure whether the self-identification of the Jew is over against his neighbour or from within. (The religious Jew's answer would be, neither: it is from the God who chose his people, and it is that choice which marks him in his own eyes and his neighbour's.) But it is possible to examine the evidence of communal consensus, without pretending to certainty about its ultimate meaning. There is, for example, a good deal of tolerance in deed, among the intolerant words. Neturei Karta, the irreconcilables, are tacitly given complete exemption from any law to which they object: they are free of the obligations of military service and school attendance. After his retirement Ben-Gurion wrote in defence of *laissez faire* in the matter of the zealot sect's attacks on tourists:

It is always more difficult when acts are prompted by a deep religious belief . . . they represent a world most of us come from

... they look like our grandfathers. How can you slap your
grandfather into jail, even if he throws stones at you? ... There is
also a political aspect ... the religious parties in the coalition ...
are in agreement with some of the demands of Neturei Karta ...
they would find it hard to remain as partners in a government
that took strong action against a group that fought, even illegally,
for Sabbath observance.[8]

The extreme Hasidic sect of the Lubavitsche has a village, Habad,
which lies almost in what would have been the direct line of the motor-
way between Jerusalem and Tel Aviv. This is used, naturally, seven days
a week. Sabbath driving at the edge of the village would be an offence:
the road was bent. The cars would still have been visible: a high
wattle fence was erected. Of course the villagers know they are there:
to suspend visual imagination is their contribution to communal unity.
Again, the Agudat Israel party, only less extreme than Neturei Karta,
fought fiercely against the construction of a municipal pool in
Jerusalem in which there is mixed bathing, and on the Sabbath. Now,
as supporters of the Coalition Government, they withdraw from the
Knesset annually while funds for the public water supply are voted. If
these picturesque trivia did not express a deeper solidarity they would
not be worth recording. But they are in their way illustrative of the
strong threads that tie together the ideologically sundered elements.
A number of religious thinkers discount both the division itself and the
'secularity' of the seculars, whom they see as more religious than they
themselves realize. 'If they lived abroad they'd wake up to their real
attitudes.' There may be some wishful thinking here, but a germ of
truth too. At a public gathering in Jerusalem Adin Steinsalz, an
orthodox rabbi and scholar, referring to Israel's most famous states-
man, pointed out that 'for Mr Ben-Gurion we are a chosen people –
chosen by a God he doesn't believe in, for reasons he denies, in a Book
he doesn't accept'. Sharp, penetrating words: a taunt that might almost
have been a compliment. Again, let us recall the Government's action
in reversing the Supreme Court's decision in the Schalit case and
restoring the religious definition of a Jew. The Prime Minister introducing the crucial amendment spoke as a known agnostic, who was
nevertheless convinced that religion was the indispensable cement of
Jewish unity. Indeed, she felt its binding force herself.

In present-day Russia, where regular Jewish association is impossible, the synagogue is the sole unifying force for the youth,

however little they understand its significance. I often felt while in Moscow [in 1948, as Israel's Minister] that if I had stayed much longer I would have gone to synagogue out of conviction, and not out of obligation as a diplomat.

It is possible to classify both Mrs Meir and Ben-Gurion as members of an older generation of 'seculars' whose nostalgic links with the Jewish past are a vanishing factor, not typical of younger leaders or the population at large. On the other hand there is evidence that their attitudes owe more to a sense of continuing realities than to nostalgia. Ben-Gurion's two-edged reference to Neturei Karta and his remarks about kosher kitchens have been quoted. Mrs Meir's words rallied the support of a large majority in the Knesset for her amendment, and her speech included a pointed reference to another powerful factor making for cohesion and unified action in the State. She said that the time had not yet come 'when we here in Israel with our two and a half million Jews can tranquilly accept the thesis that the existence of Jewry is not threatened. We are faced with a great and very substantial danger from assimilation.' The proportion of intermarriage among American Jews was 20 per cent. 'I do not support this law for the sake of Government unity, or the welfare of the religious parties. Nor do I believe that if it is passed, intermarriage will cease in the Diaspora. But at least the Diaspora will know that Israel has not established a licence to inter-marriage.'

The Prime Minister's speech thus contained three elements of long term significance. She implied that without its religious tie the survival of the Jewish people was uncertain. She made it clear that in a hostile environment (Moscow, in her case) she herself found that her Jewish sentiment rested on a basis to which her reason did not need to give consent. Finally, she acknowledged Israel's bond with the Jews of the Diaspora in a partnership of mutual care and concern. To some of the ablest men in Israel the speech and the outcome pointed to an almost miraculous element, under the political surface. Through the mouth of a secular Prime Minister, with the support of parties of the left far more doctrinaire in their historical materialism than the British Labour Party, (which goes to church at party conferences and hears its leader read the lesson) a point essential to religious Jewry had been won. Another and altogether more mundane interpretation is possible. But that misses the point, which is the ultimate coincidence of religious and secular reasoning and attitudes, in a common acceptance of the unity of the Jewish people as fundamental. There is, naturally, a political dimension to this unity, and it goes deeper than the simple bargaining which keeps the Israel Labour and Religious Parties together by mutual concessions from each to the other's essential interests. For much of the Knesset's life, the religious parties' support has not been necessary for a Coalition majority. The solidarity is of a different kind. As the author was told in Israel, 'The religious parties put pressure on the Cabinet, the Rabbinate puts pressure on the religious parties, Neturei Karta puts pressure on the Rabbinate, and the Satmar Rebbe [Neturei Karta's spiritual leader in Brooklyn] puts pressure on Neturei Karta.' The secret begins with a chain of partially shared fundamentalist convictions, and culminates in the unwillingness of the Cabinet's secular majority – several times illustrated in these pages – to coerce a Jewish religious minority by the secular power of a Jewish State. The intensity of secular conviction is reserved for matters outside the field of orthodox belief. Who would split the community in the name of his belief that the Jewish people are *not* the chosen of God, that there is *no* cosmic drama with Israel playing the lead, that the salvation of mankind does *not* depend on the fulfilment of God's purpose to raise up Israel as a light to the gentiles? How many seculars in Israel, looking about the western world, are likely to discern among its spiritual wreckage the light that they could hold up, to outshine the beam of the traditional faith?

Meanwhile the voice of that faith does not waver. In the correspondence already referred to Dr Harold Fisch wrote of

> the profounder unity at work below the surface uniting the whole people in its covenant destiny in spite of the struggle between the so-called religious and secular elements and the unceasing search for identity that is going on. We are – paradoxical as it might sound – one people. Never was this more clearly demonstrated than at the Western Wall on 7 June 1967. We are also one people, rather a strange one at that, in finding the time and the energy to fight bitterly over the question of what is a Jew whilst the enemy stands at the gate. Surely, in this very intensity of search for meaning which is going on throughout the people we have a partial answer to the question, who is a Jew? And for those of us who have faith it seems that to such an intensity of search the answer must eventually be vouchsafed.

Self-imposed common fate, or covenant destiny?

Jewish Identity: Analytical

It is sometimes argued, and very plausibly, that the Jewish tie is familial: the hypothesis fits the facts well. You do not join a family, but are born into it. You can leave it, disown it, even in the end forget and be forgotten by it, without altering the fact of membership. While you remain in any kind of contact you can love the other members or hate them, esteem or despise them, share or reject their views. The bond remains. To suggest that it is literally as inseverable as a blood-tie would be historically false. Besides innumerable mixed unions – marriages, liaisons, rapes – Jewish history contains many large-scale examples of membership renounced or forfeit, by the slow process of assimilation, or with the speed of voluntary or forced conversion. There was a mad logic in Hitler's 'final solution': if it is really essential that Jewish blood shall not infiltrate the entire community, the only course is to destroy its possessors. Yet even that would be too late. After a hundred generations there can be few families in lands where Jews have ever lived who can be sure of an ancestry completely *judenrein* and few, if any, Jews whose line goes back with no gentile intervention to the congregation in Solomon's temple. But this huge Jewish legion of the lost has no real meaning. It is the faithful remnant that makes Jewry, preserves it and transmits its character. This is the 'family'.

There are Israelis who disavow it, who deny that their Jewishness has any meaning. They are content to be citizens of a nation like other nations. They owe nothing – they feel – to their Jewish past except the fact that it has brought them to where they are and given them the chance to think of it as just another national history which happens to be their own. We heard their voices in the 'conversations among young people': 'Jewry is finished, having completed its role. We have now the State of Israel. . . . We defend our country as Israelis.' Again, 'The main thing is to live. What's the difference what culture, which tradition?' This rootless group-membership is not a negligible feature in the life of the State, either in numbers or potential influence. If it became much more widespread it might in time grow some levantine character and personality of its own. To echo Justice Silberg's words, it was not for that purpose that the pioneers undertook the task of spreading the great doctrine of Zionism. But it need not concern us further here, because its answer to the question that heads this section of the book is that a Jew is no longer anything. It denies or ignores everything and anything that the majority believes to be the secret of the family bond.

What then is that secret? What do Jews themselves think it is? Digging down through things heard, read and seen brings to view four layers, mixed but distinguishable: the sense of attachment, the sense of shared history and destiny, the sense of corporate mission, and one other dimension. Let us try to penetrate them in turn, from the surface downward.

Attachment The feeling of belonging is an emotional fact of great power. The Professor of Sociology in the Hebrew University is on record as thinking it the essential criterion of Jewishness: 'The crucial test is when we feel the common bond stronger than anything else.'

For the individual, this may be a subjective test: he regards himself as a Jew if his Jewish allegiance is stronger than any competing public attachment. As the mark of a people, however, and taken by itself, it would seem to be an emotion empty of content, or with a content so varied and unstable, so open to change and distortion as to amount to no more than the very lowest common denominator of Jewishness. For the time being, the emotion has its vessels: the close inter-communication system of a very small community, where every individual soldier's death is an almost personal grief to everyone, where conversation is a uniquely large component of leisure, where the various élites – military, political, academic, artistic, commercial – mingle and interchange ideas intimately and continuously in an idiom permeated with the symbolism of the Bible, where the Land itself and its ruins and relics are an ever present reminder of the ancient bond.

Yet such vessels of themselves give no permanence to the quality of the emotion, no fixed content. The tinge of Jewishness may seem unfading today: but if emotional attachment were all, a few decades of unforeseeable change could tune out the colour from the picture and leave only the black-and-white of 'normal' secular nationalism. Attachment is a strong link but not of itself meaningful therefore not inherently secure; this is plain to many thoughtful Israelis young and old, and they say so.

History and Destiny The sense of a shared past and a shared future takes us nearer the heart of the matter. Of those who, without being religious, think seriously about their Jewishness, the largest number appear to accept the mark of the Tradition. This is much more than a shared set of memories of exile endured and persecution survived. If it were only that, it could be just an old and bloody story to be expunged from emotion if not from memory, and to be remembered without pride. But we are speaking of something deeper and more characteristic, the sense of Time, the feel of Time in the blood.

Up from the wilderness, out from the tents –
                . . . the formidable
incarnation of the continuity of a tribe.
                    You move, inaccessible,
through a tissue of time: through a landscape of the mind
so vehemently composed – so blazed in the skull and viscera-known –
that in very truth these stones underfoot
    must have, for you, the feel of bones
and this breathed air (for me no more than everywhere air)
be the densed breath, still hot and strong, of all who have passed
this turbulent way, since the search began. . . .
There is nowhere to hide:
    in the whole enormous splendor of sun
nowhere to escape from what has been! The deeds tower, sinewing
    space;
the words beat through like a giant pulse. And this white dust,
this blinding dazzle of powdered past, has a terrible power
to enthrall whoever attends to dust,
    being vision, anguish, vengeance, loss. . . .
Under each step
    lie the packed passions of three thousand years.[1]

Early in 1970 there appeared in the magazine of the Kibbutz movements an article by a member of Kibbutz Haon, a secular Kibbutz, which sums up in straightforward terms a widespread sentiment. This is an extract:

If I were to stop a friend and ask him: 'What is your right to this country you live in, and what of the nation you drive out in

the name of just wars?' He would probably answer: 'My right is
a historical right, my ancestors' right'. And if I were to ask
further 'Who were your ancestors?' 'David, Solomon, the
Hasmoneans, etc., a splendid line of revered heroes.' 'What, from
that time to this day? Is it possible for a man to be descended
from ancestors who lived two thousand years ago?' So it becomes
plain that we are in fact descendants of Menachem Mendel,
Benjamin the Third, Tuvia the milkman [popular figures from
modern Hebrew writings] and other names.

It is true that even if a son turns his back on his father, he is
still a son of that father. But does the same apply to a nation?
Given the existence of a gulf of ignorance and alienation between
us and Judaism, meaning Jews in the Diaspora and religious Jewry
here in Israel, is our right to the heritage still valid? And if,
indeed, we are Jews, in what ways? Is it because we happened to
be born to fathers who in turn were also brought unwillingly into
the covenant of Abraham our forefather? Or perhaps we bought
our right by living in the promised land? (But then Arabs and
Christians live here too.) It is convenient for us to disregard these
problems and create a new culture in a new country as if there
has been nothing here before, or as if what did exist was no
concern of ours. But it seems to me that we thus lose not only
unmatched and unmatchable cultural riches, but lose also the basis
of our existence and the justification of our struggle. The only
conclusion is that we must try and bring ourselves closer to these
cultural riches and remove the barrier of alienation which
separates us from them.

The efforts to 'remove the barrier' are quite widespread, as we have
seen. But their form and intensity differ. They range from celebrating
the historic festivals in an almost entirely secular spirit (like the Christ-
mas tree in a pagan household in the West) to a serious – though
uncommitted – search for deeper meaning in the historic record and
the teachings of the Bible and Talmud. As the Kibbutznik said, 'In
their search for the "Old Jewish culture" perhaps they will drink some
spiritual living water from the well of culture'. But there are plenty
who have a feeling for cultural tradition yet stay well on the secular
side, giving no recognition or acceptance to the force that created the
tradition. Dr Eliezer Schweid of the Hebrew University has written:

What remains of Tradition once its original quality is forced to abdicate? Shreds of custom and folklore! . . . On the other hand, what remains of a culture the specific quality of which rests in religion, once religion has been expelled? A language and a little literature and custom, which too are donning alien vestments. Is such a culture, impervious to its own origins and sources notwithstanding the attraction they still possess for it, capable of halting the process of polarization and disintegration?[2]

And the 'spiritual living water'? How far the exploration of tradition will take the more serious diviners may depend in part on the way it is presented to them. If it appears as the embodiment of a rigid, allembracing rule of observance it is liable to repel the great majority. The studies and investigations of the young secular Kibbutzniks must at some stage bring them to the point where the full rigour of the code would demand their acceptance: and some of those who know them best doubt if more than a handful would accept it. Under that challenge the current signs of return to Tradition might turn out no more than a passing phase. But it may be the rigidity of the code itself which proves to belong to a past that has no future. He would be a bold observer who would add such a forecast to the many made and disproved in the past. Yet there is something paradoxical in the idea of a religion that makes history central but would deny change. Indeed we have already found reason to doubt whether in its normal condition Judaism does resist change. Outside the religious establishment and its least reflective adherents, few in Israel today would argue that it does.

In 1963 there was a discussion between one of the most eminent of Jewish scholars, Professor Gershom Scholem of the Hebrew University, (author of the modern classic: *Jewish Mysticism*) and a group of high-school teachers who sought his help in conveying to their students the meaning of the Jewish heritage. It was reported in summary form in the magazine *Prozdor*.[3] He told them

emphatically that there is no definitive answer to the question 'What is Judaism?' Judaism as a religious phenomenon is a vast complex of ideas and beliefs which has undergone continuous change and development throughout the ages . . . it will continue to change as long as it remains a vital religion. This vital and living force [is] the 'Utopian aspects' of the Jewish past and future which have as yet not been revealed. No two generations of Jews have ever conceived Judaism in the same way, for each generation has defined Judaism in terms of its own specific situation.

(One wonders what a teenager in high-school, hot for certainties, would make of that.)

Even Leon Roth, a scholar of impeccable orthodoxy, writes: 'The only authority in matters of belief in Judaism is that of factual acceptance, and this has varied, at least in precision and emphasis, in different environments and different ages.'[4] Of the Talmud: 'Every generation has its own needs and its own wise men to meet them, and every teacher and student has its own language and style.'[5] In the pages of the journal *Petahim*[6] the editor, Joseph Bentwich, distinguishes 'between Mitzvah (the idea of an absolute moral duty) and Mitzvot (the detailed laws and observances)'. Using as analogy the development of the law in a modern state, he points out that besides precedent the judge will take account not only of legal history, to show that a given precedent referred to a different form of society, but of contemporary ideas of justice and morality, and finally of the requirements of reason and consistency. He then himself quotes the august precedent of the Talmud itself:

> Rav Tsa'ir (Chernovitz) in tracing the history of the Halakhah, also emphasizes its developmental character. The rabbis were by no means bound by precedent or by the Written Law, but would often use their reason to derive new principles. In so doing they would follow the *spirit*, rather than the letter of the Law; and they would take into account the needs of the hour. . . . Throughout, they would have to consider popular feelings and values. 'An injunction of the court, which is not accepted by the majority of the people, is not valid.' (*Yerushalmi* Shabbat).

Then, the voice of orthodox scholarship itself – that of the Rector of the religious University of Bar-Ilan.

> It is true that the Oral Law which is a dynamic developing system has been for some time in the deep freeze. But if I say to you that this will not last forever and that sooner or later in response to the stresses of history it will become alive and mobile once again, I do not merely cease to be an authentic (or, in your term, Orthodox) Jew. On the contrary I attach myself to classical Jewish categories which relate Jewish existence as much to the future as to the past. Judaism is committed to the notion of an

ongoing historical process, of a redemptive change to come and of a new heaven and a new earth. . . . Ezekiel's vision of the dry bones, lies deep in the consciousness of all Jews, even those whose bones are dry, and we live in the expectation of a reviving wind to come.[7]

There was also another Prophet, who wrote: 'For there is still a vision for the appointed time. At the destined hour it will come in breathless haste, it will not fail. If it delays, wait for it, for when it comes will be no time to linger.'[8]

No one can tell whether or when secular will yield to spiritual vision. But in Israel, waiting is an active process. To consider the motive power behind the activity is the next step towards the heart of the secret.

Mission 'The Chosen' is what some gentiles, echoing Christian theology, call the Jewish people. The usage is not always kindly in spirit, but it is shrewd in its perception that this astonishing claim is historically the mark of Jewish identity as Jews themselves have seen it. If we accept the biblical evidence, and on this point archaeology in its latest phase no longer discredits it, the idea did not develop from a primitive tribal myth to a more exalted conception, but had from the outset – from Father Abram's setting forth – two aspects: particular nationhood and the universal idea. ('I will make of thee a great nation . . . and thou shalt be a blessing.') The Mission of Israel has been both a mission to itself and a mission to 'the nations', each of the two the condition of the other's fulfilment. The meaning of this to the orthodox Jew calls for no further elaboration: our purpose is to consider the light it throws on the mystery of Jewish identity in a secular state where the orthodox are a minority.

In all Jewish history, considered simply as a secular record of the life of a certain people, there is a quality of restless driving, a discontent, a reaching forward, an inbuilt messianism. The Professor of Modern Jewish History in the Hebrew University puts it admirably:

Imbued from the beginning of their history as a people with the idea that they must accept a particularly heavy yoke or responsibility because they were charged with the mission of serving as a light unto the nations, the Jews were *incapable of finding meaning in a life strictly devoted to the here and now* and lacking any transcendental significance. . . . Zionism on its face had called for the 'normalization' of the Jewish people but it could never bring that about. An abnormal people, the Jews are driven. Strive they must, justify themselves in their own eyes and in the eyes of others they must. They are unable to take reality as it is for granted. They are hypnotized, now as always, by *the idea of ultimate meaning*, final dénouement.[9]

The language is impeccably secular: the message between the lines is the continuing force of the Covenant and the Mission. What expression do these find in the contemporary life of Israel?

For one thing, there is a continuing corporate self-judgment, an intense and widespread preoccupation with the moral standard of performance of the community as a community, the people as a people. The tension of its life under continued military threat is no explanation of this. In the talk of the young men, first as soldiers then as Kibbutz workers, there was sensitiveness to ethical values, self-questioning whether a war for Jewish survival could be fought by standards that would leave to survival its meaning, concern for justice, care for civilian life regardless of whether the civilian was Jew or Arab, a tendency at the moment of conquest to identify with the victim. We found it also in the insistence of a minority on a policy towards Arabs which did not fall short of the full measure of idealism in the teaching of Judaism. The minority was significantly large, when one remembers that it was not moved by war-weariness or frustration but by an ideal that claimed allegiance even under the continuing threat to the nation's survival. What moved it was the ingrained belief, born of the tradition of revelation *to a people*, that in a corrupt society there can be no full individual salvation. There is also a more obviously constructive aspect of the sense of mission, visible in what Buber called 'the age-old Jewish longing to incorporate social truth in the lives of individuals living with one another'. One saw it in the aspiration of the young Ben-Gurion to create a 'model society, which could become, in the language of the Biblical Prophets, a light unto the nations'. It is to be seen in the communal patterns that we have examined: in the social institutions of labour-Zionism, in the Kibbutz, the only successful Utopia so far realized, in the Army, the military machine that is also a civil crusader, in the Ingathering, the deliberate subordination of other political, social and economic goals to the ideal of unity and equality – that is, the unity and equality of Jews.

There is also the relation of trust and confidence built up with a large number of economically backward countries in Africa and Asia, a relation based on practical help, disinterested and comradely enough in spirit to have avoided the usual sour penalties of international beneficence.

This last example looks outward. But in the main, in Israel today, the corporate self-judgment shows as its obverse a self-preoccupation: the dedication is to a nationally bounded standard of corporate achievement: the mission is inward. It is the hazard of the sense of election that it must seem to tremble always on the brink of corporate egotism. Consider the following paragraph, quoted from a writer in *Petahim*, and selected because it is not singular but fairly representative of an attitude held consciously by a number and unconsciously by many more:

> The world is in need of mending more than ever before. The powers of corruption have increased tenfold with the increased powers of technology. It would seem that Western civilisation is coming to an end. Is it conceivable that a small people of 15 million can bring about a rebirth? Yes! – because we are still the people of the *Covenant*, the Covenant between man and God. We are the 'guardians'. And now we are called to be true to our task.

Some latitude, some lapse from objectivity, is allowed to a general addressing his troops before battle. But this is a spiritual struggle; if the spirit of the battle address fell short, the outcome would be prejudiced.

The Jews have given to the civilized world a universal moral code of individual conduct: the world accepts it as an ideal standard, and Jews themselves have, measured by the standard of human achievement, lived up to it at least as well as any people. But the other half of the message is a code of social and communal conduct, to be embodied concretely and fully in a way of life. This embodiment – so the message runs – must be achieved in Israel because it includes many aspects of life, from the conduct of international relations to the use of a police force, in which responsibility can be exercised only by a community that governs itself and grapples for itself with the moral issues involved in the exercise of power. The nations of the world have no such code: Jewish thinkers criticize the Christian ethic because it has provided none, and does not go beyond the concept of salvation as individual. The world surely needs such a code if it can be found. What is to be the witness of the State of Israel?

Two questions force themselves upon the mind. One is simple and practical, the other complex and more profound. First, can a comprehensive way of life be defined and practised in a divided community? When the code was formulated between sixteen and twenty centuries ago, it was by spiritual leaders whose authority was unquestioned, who lived and taught against a background of common belief about essentials. Where today is the focus of authority? Where the consensus? The world of non-communist states has a different answer. It has settled for democratic pluralism, and does not merely accept it as a *pis aller* but defends it as a true recognition of the unlimited potentialities of free growth. For practical purposes, in Israel as it is, what more has the doctrine of corporate mission to add?

The second question goes to the root of the idea of a national religion. In a world of nation states, living amid the dire perils of a condition of international anarchy limited only by the expediencies of self-interest, can a universal witness be borne by the people of a separate state with its own existence to defend? It can behave decently: any civilized state can do as much. But can spiritual witness to universal justice and truth be borne by a separatist example? Can the universal mission of Israel in this day and age be carried out by a national 'pilot model'? Is not the witness the world needs that of the ability to transcend nationalism, yet stay alive?

There is here a dilemma. A nation seeking to live the life of the spirit must grapple with its corporate tasks: without political responsibility it is but a shadow witness. Yet if it lives as the nations do, with only their own wills for a law, can it survive except as other nations do?

There are powerful reasons for the existence of a Jewish state. Is the idea of a *national* mission a valid one? Only the people of Israel, within or beyond their state, can answer.

The other dimension Any attempt to define Jewish identity runs the risk of either slipping into, or being misunderstood as, an analysis of the conscious attitude of Jews, which must be wrong if it is not applicable at least to most of them. Clearly there are thoughtful atheist Jews who are relaxed and happy, just as there are Sabbath sunbathers on the beach at Herzliya permanently untroubled by spiritual questions. Here we are trying to define a norm, the animating principle of Jewishness. For this, one flies in the face of evidence historical and contemporary unless one includes in the norm awareness and acknowledgment of transcendent power: a faith in God which is not asserted because it is presupposed.

There is a story that has been going the rounds in Israel for at least a decade. The author heard it newly dressed in fresh academic robes, but its essence appeared in print as long ago as 1961.[10] It concerns a secular student of religious forms arguing with a believer, who finally asks, 'But why do you never mention God, in all you say?' and gets the reply, 'What has God to do with religion?' This little tale has two points. One is the obsessive concern in all public controversy and much private argument with observance, the outward aspect of religion. The other is that the sense of transcendent spiritual power, in the thought of the people who first felt and expressed it, is still present and operative in the minds of many who do not consciously acknowledge it. It is there, as the air is there whether or not one is aware of inspiration. The records of Jewish life, writing and achievement are not wholly explicable on any other assumption. Nor indeed is the sense of mission itself, unless one is prepared to call it no more than the projection of an insatiable need to lay down the law. And that seems an inadequate account of how the Psalms got written, or Isaiah, or the Book of Job, or why a people has for thousands of years found in them the meaning of life. Here is the deepest layer. Here is the contact with ultimate truth, where moral teaching and moral impulsion are rooted.

The awareness may be unseeing, as it is in the restlessness of which we have taken note, in the constant widespread emphasis on striving and searching. There is a Hasidic tale worth recalling. It concerns a Hasid who complained to the Rabbi of Kotzk:

'Rabbi,' he said, 'I am given to so much contemplation that I find no peace.'

'And what is it that you are forced to contemplate about?' the Rabbi asked.

'I am forced to ponder the question whether there is truly a judge and judgment in the world.'

'And why should you care?'

'Rabbi,' he said, 'if there is neither judgment nor judge, to what purpose is Creation?'

'And why should you care?'

'Rabbi, if there is neither judge nor judgment what sense is there in the words of the Torah?'

'And why should you care?'

'What say you, Rabbi? What else should I care about?'

'If you really care so much about it,' the Rabbi replied, 'you

are a good Jew and a good Jew may ponder those questions
without fear of his belief being weakened,'

or (one might dare to paraphrase) without condemning himself for
losing touch with God.

Perhaps closer to the age-long continuity of the practice of Judaism
is the spiritual life of what Ernst Simon has called 'the classical modest
Jewish religious type ... leading its daily life sanctified by God,
without, except in prayer, overly mentioning God's name'.[11]

In the same essay he refers again to this 'hard core of the people ...
proceeding on its way, under the familiar burden of the law' and he
speaks of its characteristic reticence about the divine in the charming
phrase 'the religious chastity of silence'.

At the other end of the scale is the mystical strain in Jewish religious
thought, which in the eighteenth century found fresh embodiment in
the movement called Hasidism, or Pietism. By its nature mysticism is
not easily described, and the primary materials are for scholars. Buber
wrote much about it, and Gershom Scholem in his *Jewish Mysticism*[12]
has provided a brilliantly clear and compendious account. For the
present purpose the essence of what he writes is:

> The originality of Hasidism lies in the fact that the mystics who
> had attained their spiritual aim ... turned to the people with their
> mystical knowledge ... and instead of cherishing as a mystery the
> most personal of all experiences, undertook to teach its secret to
> all men of goodwill.

Again:

> The true originality of Hasidic thought is to be found here and
> nowhere else. As mystical moralists the Hasidim found a way to
> social organisation. Again we see the ancient paradox of solitude
> and communion. He who has attained the highest degree of
> spiritual solitude, who is capable of being alone with God, is the
> true centre of the community, because he has reached the stage at
> which true communion becomes possible.

At this point, where inward vision and outward expression identify at
a level far above the observance of a ritual code, we are surely in
touch with one of the highest expressions of Judaism. It is to be
remembered too that an earlier Jewish teacher with the gift of spiritual
communion had from the whole vast aggregate of the Torah culled

and coupled just these two, the love of God and of neighbour, as the greatest of the Mitzvot.[13] Like him, like other Jews of his time,[14] and like at least one of the Tannaite rabbis late in the first century AD[15] the Hasid sages – the greatest of them – carried their spiritual witness to the point where their prayers healed the sick.

Scholem thinks that today Hasidism is in decay, but alive and capable of revival in some unpredictable way. It is certainly on view in Israel, but even in its liveliest and most outgoing form (Habad Hasidism, the sect of the Lubavitsche) it shows no sign of any outreach beyond the bounds of the Jewish community. Nor did the movement at its spiritual height. Communion with God, though God is One, made the communicant the centre only of the Jewish community. This was true of the great Hasidic sages. It was true also of their greatest recent successor, the Palestine Chief Rabbi Abraham Isaac Kook: not technically a Hasid but a saint and mystic greatly influenced by their thought, and like the Hasid sages a teacher and man of affairs. It is in his writings (voluminous but hard for any but scholars to reach) that the sense of the presence of God, and of the Mission of Israel, are brought most closely into unison. Kook saw danger in any premature universalism: his vision of God was mirrored in a vision of the ideal people of Israel. He saw that ideal as real and present behind the surface show of imperfection. In S. H. Bergman's words:

> To him Israel is what its name signifies: a warrior of God, a people which has taken upon itself the task to battle for God and which therefore feels responsible for the fate of the divine in the world. This struggle for God and against death is nothing less than the struggle for a new form of consciousness freed from the illusion that death is a reality. No defeat can discourage him who feels called to share in the struggle. Death is an imperfection of creation and Israel's task is to remove it.[16]

Kook believed that their life in alien lands had separated Jews from the spring of holiness, which would flow again in Palestine. He knew that return would be beset with difficulties and that these would bring the temptation to act 'like other nations'. In his words: 'It is proper to nurture national honour and seek to enhance it; but national honour is not an end in itself. It can only be the by-product of the realisation of our most important task: to testify and be witness in the world to the name and glory of God.' Again: 'Israel will not complete its historic journey in a storm; God is not to be found in the raging tempest; He can be found only in the small voice. Israel must not raise her voice in anger or aggressiveness to the outside world. Nevertheless, in the words of the prophets, "The isles will wait for her teaching".' These are the words of Isaiah (42:4) as rendered in the English translation of Bergman's book. In the Authorized Version they wear the more familiar form 'The isles shall wait for his law'. The reference is to the 'suffering servant' who stands in the Jewish interpretation for the people of Israel itself. Thus Kook's messianic vision takes the form that lies at the very heart of traditional Judaism – the message of redemption through suffering, of obedience to a God whose will for man, good in some ultimate inscrutable sense, may demand of him now an indefinite endurance of evil. This is the 'Jewish value' that the religious accept and the secular reject. It marks as we have seen the difference between the young who turn away repelled from the spirit of the ghetto and those for whom that is an essential part of the teaching of Judaism, between those who look for protection from future holocausts to the Israeli army and those who look beyond that to the power of a Spirit which may demand even a sacrifice of national purpose. To put it in Kook's terms, suppose that the tempest rages again and the still small voice is not soon heard? It has happened before, and residence in the Land of Israel has not prevented it.

Kook wrote before the holocaust had made the *total* annihilation of a people an evident possibility, and at a time when it was reasonable to think that non-resistance might end in the survival of at least a remnant. Now, in the armed State of Israel, enmeshed in the calculus of power, there can be very very few religious people, aside from Neturei Karta, who believe that their duty under the Covenant could call them like lambs to the slaughter, or even require them to accept the abolition of their State so that the People and its Faith could survive. That decision is made. Nor can they find reason in history or experience to trust to 'the conscience of mankind'. For practical purposes, the State has become an ultimate value: whatever else the Israeli Jew may be, he is in this sense a Zionist.

Yet within the limits thus set there are still choices to be made. Pacifist self-surrender is ruled out, and with it that much of the ghetto's imposed rule of life. In Israel they 'have the power, and they would slay'. But at what point, and for what? Whither does the spirit of the ancestral teaching point the Jew? Perhaps it points him first to problems he himself is free to solve: the situation of his Arab fellow citizens and of the refugees dispossessed by their fears of him and by his needs.

Here he has much to give, at every level. And if he moved in that direction it might lead him nearer to ground on which he and his embattled neighbours could meet. Perhaps God waits for Israel in the stranger's tent.

There is a Biblical story whose meaning is constantly at work in the imagination of Jews who know their history. It is the tale of the sacrifice of Isaac, whom his father Abraham was ready to offer up at the command of the God who was testing him. Here are two reactions to it as recounted to the author.

A young soldier in the Sinai campaign of 1956 was given a 'suicide mission', to start in three days. He spent those days convinced, as Isaac may have been during that other desert journey to Mount Moriah, that his life was at an end. He saw himself as Isaac, asked himself what that God could be who would demand such a sacrifice, and told himself rebelliously that it could not be right to serve Him. As a soldier, then and there, he had no choice. But that did not settle the spiritual issue, either for him or for those who might in the future be free to choose between 'staying in Israel to be killed' or 'going to America to watch TV'. On the third day the mission was called off. When he was past the phase of overwhelming, unthinking relief, he resumed his reflections. He too had been reprieved. Perhaps the meaning was that if one trusted and endured, the penalty would be remitted. If one lived as Isaac, one might 'end up as Abraham'. *Hinneni*. Here am I.

There was a schoolboy, escaped to Israel with his family from the torture and horror of the camps in Germany into which they had been shepherded by the Nazis. He knew little or nothing of the Bible, and the Isaac story, imaginatively told, broke in upon his mind with a sense of terrible reality. From his questions and comments it was clear to his teacher that he saw himself not as the helpless Isaac but as the man, Abraham, who had to decide. At the end he rose in his desk and struck it hard with his open hand three times, shouting loudly, 'I wouldn't have gone! I wouldn't have gone! I wouldn't have gone!'

Here are the two sides to the mind and nature of the people of the State of Israel. This is the enigma of Jewish identity. Can either side be the 'right' one? Can both be? Job seemed to think so and Job is a very Jewish book: 'Though he slay me, yet will I trust in him: but I will maintain my own ways before him.' In the end he found his reconciliation by simple surrender, which is not a full answer since according to the narrative it was a surrender to superior power. Job's vision was from within a material universe, whose lawless force seemed to him the will of the Lord. The voice he heard spoke out of the whirlwind. He did not challenge it in the name of a still, small voice that is at once supreme goodness and supreme power. On what terms Israel is to find its full reconciliation, after what illusions shed, what dear convictions yielded up, is the question that remains. Rabbi Kook had a glimpse of the answer: how far that answer can be valid within the limits of his own national approach is the central question on which this book seeks to throw a little light.

Appendix

Appendix

Some Notes on Israel as a Factor in Jewish-Christian Relations

The modest purpose of these notes is to draw attention to some changes in the relations between the two great western religions as occasioned or affected by the existence of Israel. Where possible the points are made in the words of local participants or commentators.

> A question affecting two world religions thought to have been settled nearly two thousand years ago has once more been re-opened. . . . The parting of the Church and the Synagogue that was for all intents and purposes accepted in the second century has once more been questioned in the twentieth century.

Peter Schneider (see p 174)

So wrote the Christian clergyman who advises the Anglican Archbishop in Jerusalem on Jewish-Christian relations. Thus modestly expressed, in terms of a question reopened, the assertion is beyond argument. What may come of it is another matter. But to understand how great a step forward is the mere admission that there is enough common ground to make genuine dialogue possible, one needs to recall what were for eighteen centuries the official positions. The Church proclaimed that it had taken over everything good in Judaism, leaving a faithless people to suffer endless penalty in witness of the fate of deicides. Israel and Jerusalem had lost their status as historic realities and become idealized as the (Christian) people of God and the (Christian) Kingdom of Heaven. To Jews, Christianity began as the creed of a sect of heretics, of no great importance once cast out; then became the banner of a vast mixed tribe which slaughtered Jews in the name of a religion of love. Medieval Jewish law about gentiles, in reaction to the brutal harshness of 'Christian' law about Jews, matched it in severity (of course one was theory, the other practice). Doctrinally, conventional Christian theology, of any orthodox school, seems to many Jewish thinkers to fall below the level of pure spiritual monotheism: the idea that Christianity is an idolatrous mixture persists.

It was Christian scholarship which moved first, and most significantly. An English unitarian, R. Travers Herford, who wrote during
the second and third decades of this century, began by unearthing all
the references to Christians and Christianity in the Talmud and
Midrash, throwing much light on the common background. He then
went on in later writings to demonstrate the lofty ethical quality of
Pharisaical teaching, bring out the fact that Jesus' denunciations of
hypocrisy and excessive legalism could all be matched or outmatched
in the rabbis' own utterances, and suggest that what was in essence a
breach within the family had been completely distorted into a declaration of war on Judaism, with disastrous effects for Christianity and
for Jews. Then came an American, the Professor of the History of
Religion at Harvard, George Foot Moore, whose monumental work
Judaism in the First Centuries of the Christian Era (1927) broadly confirmed Herford's view, showed the very considerable resemblances
between the teaching of the Gospels and the rabbis, and argued
persuasively that though the self-righteous legalism pilloried in the
Gospels may well have existed (as self-righteousness and materialism
exist to be pilloried by a prophet in the churches of today) it could not
have been the core of rabbinical belief and teaching, because it could not
have created against massive odds a Jewish community with unique
spiritual vitality and power of survival. The Professor of the History of
Christianity at the Sorbonne, Charles Guignebert, in his *Jewish World
in the Time of Jesus*,[1] painted a similar picture, as have a number of other
Christian scholars. Notable among these is the series of books which
represent the life work of an Anglican clergyman, James W. Parkes,
whose studies of the inter-relation of Church and Synagogue are
explicitly aimed at rebutting the conventional view held by the
Christian churches, and establishing an equal and complementary
status for the two religions.

There was a corresponding development of thought on the Jewish
side in the work of Joseph Klausner, whose book *Jesus of Nazareth*[2]
made a considerable impact in the '20s by depicting Jesus as an orthodox
Jew. Klausner produced a scholarly mass of evidence to support his
interpretation, which was then something of a novelty in the Jewish
world. Dissident Jewish thinkers like Claude G. Montefiore, a pillar of
Liberal Judaism in Britain, were beginning to write on similar lines.
But after Klausner there was an interval before orthodox scholarship
turned in the same direction. Nor should it be imagined that ordinary
Christian opinions and attitudes were much influenced by the work of

the historians and analysts. The cruder ideas that had long marked Christian thought, both Roman Catholic and Protestant, have proved remarkably persistent. Among the mildest and least dangerous is the state of mind revealed by the Anglican lady who exclaimed after her first synagogue visit, 'They even use our Psalms!' A more serious cause of misunderstanding is the long-lasting inability of a good many Christian clergy and laymen, some learned and otherwise broadminded, to look at the Jewish people in its contemporary situation except through the lenses of Pauline theology as traditionally interpreted.

This type of hard-line hard-edged denominationalism is not all on one side. Professor Yeshaya Leibowitz of the Hebrew University considers that any theological *rapprochement* of Judaism and Christianity would be a radical error. He calls Goethe to witness in support of the view that Christianity belongs with paganism (Hellenism) and against Judaism, and considers that 'a frank and sincere dialogue is possible only with a Christianity that negates Judaism openly and explicitly (such as the [gnostic] sect of Marcion) but not with a Christianity that adorns itself with the borrowed plumes of "the true Judaism", and claims a Christian significance for the Torah, a claim which is blasphemy in the eyes of a religious Jew'. He contrasts God's call for the sacrifice of Abraham's son with 'the God who sacrifices his only son to save mankind' and speaks of 'the abysmal contrast between a theocentric religion, for which the ultimate purpose of man is to serve God and an anthropocentric religion, for which the deity is no more than an instrument to serve in the redemption of man'. This comes from a Professor not of any branch of Judaica but of Chemistry, and he is called by some Jews a 'religious nihilist'. Nevertheless his view of the meaning of the Atonement, and his apparent conviction that the crucifixion is to be interpreted as the end of Jesus' story, are paralleled in a good many Jewish utterances heard and read – just as they are paralleled, and in a sense justified, by a great many declarations made in the name of various forms of orthodox Christianity. One of the chief obstacles in the way of greater mutual comprehension, one of the reasons for thinking that theology may not be the most hopeful meeting-ground, is that each religion is apt to base its stereotypes of the other on those features which seem most unlike itself and are most offensive to it: and each embraces some sects and sections whose opinions justify almost anything said of it by the other. The results include the crude antitheses of Law and Grace, of this-worldly Judaism and other-worldly Christianity, of a Christian ethic that is abstract because it is individual and a Jewish code that is unspiritual because it is social, of a Christian god who is three gods over against a Jewish god who is to be served primarily by outward observance.

But even such mutual criticism has one good thing to be said for it – it is mutual. It means that after a thousand years of enduring a monologue Jews can again speak their minds about Christianity. This is the first thing that in the present context can be put to the credit of a Jewish state. In the Diaspora, emancipation did not of itself free Jews from the inhibitions that prudence imposed on a recently released minority. Nowadays the inhibitions seem to be removed and paperback invective becomes the order of the day. This change owes something to the defensive posture which world trends have imposed on the Christian churches during the last twenty years (one should remember how quickly it has happened), but in the Jewish-Christian relationship the determining fact is the appearance in the Middle East of a highly conspicuous centre of secular power and of learning.

One speaks of learning. In so far as antagonism derives from ignorance, as it partly does, learning is its cure. The various departments of Jewish study – history, philosophy, linguistics, philology, literature, archaeology, anthropology, sociology, theology – have quickly won for themselves a place of high respect in the world of scholarship. 'A growing number of Christians', says a Jerusalem newspaper article from a Christian source, 'have discovered that the Hebrew University is the place, *par excellence*, for an introduction of any depth, or for however rigorous a specialisation, in the various areas of biblical scholarship . . . the Bible, the Talmud, Hebrew Literature, the History of Israel, Jewish Philosophy and Kabbala, and Archaeology. . . . It is equally remarkable that many Christian students, Protestants in particular, follow courses in the department of Comparative Religion. To listen to lectures in which the Jewish way of interpreting the Gospel, the Church Fathers and Christian Theology is openly exposed, is both an approach to Judaism and Israel, and a particular form of dialogue.' The article lists at length the 'abundance of subjects' likely to interest the Christian historian or theologian in which courses are provided, notes the extensive programmes of one year studies in English, and records and endorses the demand for courses in French, which it says 'calls for especially weighty consideration by the University, in that there exists between the African soul and the Bible an extremely profound affinity'. (The reference is obviously to the francophone countries.) It notes the ample flow of leading Jewish scholars from the University to take classes and deliver lectures in various Christian institutes of learning in Jerusalem, and concludes by speaking of this whole development as 'one step of extreme importance towards unity between the churches in a common rediscovery of their origins and in a constructive dialogue with Israel'.[3]

The reference to 'the Jewish way of interpreting the Gospels' recalls the fact that in recent decades thoughtful Jews have turned away from the centuries' old hostile stereotypes of Jesus and accepted him as a Jewish teacher of noble stature. More specifically, the reference is in large part to the researches and writings of David Flusser, Professor of Comparative Religion. His work reflects and helps to sustain the increasing interest taken by Jews in the life and teaching of Jesus. Flusser writes in his book about him:

> Our period seems an especially appropriate one for understanding him and his preachings. A deep anxiety as to the future and the present has awakened in us a new sensitivity. We are today receptive to Jesus's revaluation of all the other values, and many of us are now becoming aware of the dubiousness of standard morality, from which awareness Jesus starts. We also, like Jesus, are feeling ourselves drawn towards the pariahs and sinners of society. . . . And if we liberate ourselves from the chains of obsolete prejudices, we are surer to respond to his demand for undivided love. . . . The tremendous achievement of his life appeals to us, also, today. . . . So we come to understand the words which, according to Matthew (28:20) he is to speak at the resurrection, in a new and unchurchly sense: 'And so, I am with you alway, even unto the end of the world.'[4]

The reference to the 'new sensitivity' awakened in us by the present state of the world recalls the title of an article 'A New Sensitivity in Judaism and the Christian Message', which Flusser wrote in the *Harvard Theological Review*, No. 61, 1968. In it he argues, with much scholarly illustration, that there was a duality in the Pharisees' attitude to God. There were Pharisees of love, and of fear (or awe). This expressed itself in controversy among the rabbis but the 'superior rating of love over awe prevailed and took hold upon all Jewish groups'. It is this that provides the background to and the link with Jesus' own teaching about love which, however, went beyond that of the Pharisees in one vital particular.

Flusser

Even if it seems probable that the moral doctrine of Jesus is influenced both by semi-Essene 'pietism' and the 'rabbinic' sensitivity, it is clear that Jesus' moral approach to God and man, even in points which are possibly influenced by others, is unique and incomparable. . . . According to the teaching of Jesus you have to love the sinners, while according to Judaism you have not to hate the wicked. It is important to note that the positive love even towards the enemies is Jesus' personal message. We do not find this doctrine in the New Testament outside of the words of Jesus himself. . . . In Judaism hatred is practically forbidden but love to the enemy is not prescribed.[5]

The article concludes with a reference to the fact that 'Christianity did not develop a specific Christian concept of social righteousness' which it did not need at the very first but now does.

From the time of Constantine until today, when Christianity became the established religion of states and societies which themselves did not originate from basic Christian concepts, a Christian answer to problems of justice, crime and punishment, and forensic morality were badly needed. Thus, Christianity always turned in such situations for help to Old Testament, or Greco-Roman solutions.

Flusser has argued both in the article under reference and elsewhere that Judaism developed and refined its ethical teaching considerably, after the Old Testament period. 'It would be a mistake to think of the Judaism of Jesus' time as being identical with the religion of the Old Testament or as being a mere development of the ancient faith of Israel.'[6] Thus his meaning is that rabbinical teaching, in its social content, supplied a need which neither the Old Testament nor the Christianity which looked to it could meet.

Christianity surpasses Judaism, at least theoretically, in its approach of love to all men, but its only genuine answer to the powerful wicked forces of this world is, as it seems, martyrdom. There is both human greatness and human weakness in our religions, but there is also the common hope for the Kingdom of Heaven.

Flusser several times expresses his view that primitive Christianity as embodied in Jesus' own life had become overlaid by later teaching and theology. It seemed to the author, in a conversation with him, that he found no difficulty in matter-of-fact acceptance of the so-called miracles of healing. He has claimed, in fact, that 'healing through the laying on of hands was practised among Jews not only by Jesus and his first disciples, but by other [and earlier] circles as well'.[7] It appears to be his view – as it is that of the Christian scholar Parkes, and others – that Jesus' own life would provide a more hopeful meeting-ground for Jewish and Christian thinkers than would later, institutionalized forms of Christianity.

Scholarship is not religion. But here are two religions in a relation of historic enmity, each claiming to derive from history and revelation, each asserting its basis in fixed codes but each in fact, and more and more undeniably, having developed and changed throughout its history. To know more about the seminal period in which one was born and parted from the other may remove the historical lumber that hides what they may have in common. When a notable scholar and teacher like Flusser, an observant Jew, declares his deeply respectful interest in the person and the special teaching of the founder of Christianity, he issues a challenge. To put it at the lowest, what he says suggests that a Jewish-Christian dialogue, on the level of scholarship, can be fruitful enough to carry agreement a little further than the courteous acknowledgment of differences which is its high point so far. Recent Christian scholarship, notably in the study of the Dead Sea Scrolls, and in uncovering the Hebrew bases of some of the Greek gospels, has taught Jews as well as Christians something new about the roots of their faiths. It would be strange if Jewish scholarship, rooted in the rabbinical teaching from which Jesus' own gospel developed, could not in its turn make a contribution of profound importance.

There are some 'ecumenical' developments. Three of those worth mentioning are the Rainbow Group of intellectuals in Jerusalem, a smaller one meeting under Christian auspices in Tel Aviv, and a Protestant Christian Kibbutz near Nahariya devoted to expressing a new Christian attitude to Judaism: they observe Shabbat, with their own Christian services, send their children to a State school, and keep in touch with their churches of origin abroad. Their relations with neighbouring Kibbutzim are good.

We conclude with a reference to the 'political' aspect of the Jewish-Christian relationship. This has always existed: it has been remarked that for most of their turbulent dual existence the Church has addressed Jews more often in terms of institutional authority than of faith. In one respect this is a little less true than it was, since the Church is less prone to regard itself as the focus of authority, and is more aware of being itself a diaspora community – an encircled minority. But in one respect only. Much of the Church has shown itself very much aware of its pastoral responsibility to Arab Christians – or as Jews would put it, has become involved with Arab nationalism to the point of being anti-Zionist and anti-Israel. It was a great shock to Jews everywhere to observe the cool aloofness with which many Christian churches reacted to what Jews regard as the blazing Arab aggression of 1967, based on repeated denials of the right of the State to exist. This led in the United States, for example, to some disruption of the superficial friendliness of the general exchanges that had been taking place. The Churches in Israel, living within the State, and finding it easier to see it as it sees itself, are themselves apt to be critical of their brethren elsewhere. The Rev. Peter Schneider, the clergyman quoted at the opening of this appendix, has written of 'dangerous superficiality and shallowness in much of the so-called ongoing Christian-Jewish dialogue in the West and . . . a serious possibility of breakdown in moments of testing and crisis', and this is by no means purely an individual opinion.

But something has changed, and the obvious explanation is that the existence of the State, and experience of its more positive qualities, are what has changed it. Even now, watchful Jews are dissatisfied: they found the Vatican Council discussions of the Deicide question incomprehensibly inconclusive, and they still think there are too few Christian voices raised in rejection of the traditional view of Israel's religion and in assertion of its independent right to its own tradition. But the development of opinion among Christians in Israel continues, and there is now some episcopal – even archiepiscopal – authority for a more genuinely fraternal attitude and approach. For one thing, the Christian practice of organized proselytization (or attempted proselytization) among Jews, for long a scandal and an offence in Jewish eyes, has been soft-pedalled, and largely abandoned. The propagandist message of Christian clergy in Israel nowadays is apt to be addressed at least as much to their own flocks as to Jews, and the aim is comprehension rather than conversion.

There is thus evidence of an increasing readiness to look at Israel, and at the Jewish people in their State, in the terms of their own identity, and not as an alien, obnoxious breed or a theological object lesson. This does not imply partisanship or unwillingness to be critical: it means rather a serious attempt to start with sympathetic appreciation and to base criticism, if any, on that. The result is that the best Christian homilies are remarkably like the best Jewish ones – demands that Israel be itself. A Dominican Father declared in August 1970, 'If we believe in the continuity of the Divine plan, of which this people was bearer and first messenger, it seems more consistent with Biblical and Gospel logic to trust in the dynamism of God's gift.'

Notes

NOTES TO CHAPTER 1, pp. 3–16

1 Martin Buber, *On Judaism*, ed. Nahum Glatzer. Schocken: New York, 1967.
2 *The Kuzari* by Jehuda Halevi. Trans., as *Kitab al Khazari*, by Hartwig Hirschfeld, pp. 44–8. Routledge: London, 1905.
3 G. F. Moore, *Judaism in the First Centuries of the Christian Era*, Vol. 1, p. 25. Italics added. Oxford University Press: London, 1927.
4 J. Goldin in *The Jews*, ed. Louis Finkelstein. O.U.P: London, 1961.
5 *New English Bible*, Deuteronomy, xxix, 14, 15.
6 *NEB*, Isaiah, lxvi, 21.
7 *NEB*, I Samuel, viii and ix.
8 *NEB*, I Chronicles, xxii, 8.

NOTES TO CHAPTER 2, pp. 17–32

1 D. Ben-Gurion, *Ben-Gurion Looks Back*, p. 33. Weidenfeld & Nicolson: London, 1969.
2 *Ibid.*, pp. 120–1.
3 Martin Buber, *Israel and the World*. Schocken: New York, 1948.
4 *NEB*, Isaiah, xix, 25.
5 There are similar utterances quoted in I. Domb, *Transformations*. Published by the author with an introduction by E. Marmorstein: London, 1958.
6 Quoted by E. Kedourie, *Nationalism*. Hutchinson: London, 1960.
7 For this remark, as for much of the material about the activities and attitudes of religious anti-Zionism in Europe and in Israel, and for several translated passages in Chapter 5, I am indebted to E. Marmorstein, *Heaven at Bay*, OUP: London, 1969. Another and less known source is *Transformations*. See note 5 above.
8 Extracted from the full text as published in Marmorstein, *op. cit.*, pp. 87–8.
9 I.e. ideological sector. See Chapter 4.
10 Ben-Gurion, *op. cit.*
11 *Ibid.*
12 The translations from Ahad Ha'am are taken from a brochure by Walter Zander, *Is this the way?* Gollancz: London, 1948, now out of print.
13 These two excerpts are quoted in the English translation of S. H. Bergman's *Faith and Reason: an Introduction to Modern Jewish Thought*. Schocken: New York, 1963.

NOTES TO CHAPTER 3, pp. 35–48

1 The tale has been told in detail by Kenneth Adam, former head of BBC TV, in *The Listener*, 4 December 1969.
2 A year before judgment was delivered the Court had asked the Government to take the issue out of the judicial province by removing the ethnic affiliation item from registration cards. This request was refused.
3 *Jerusalem Post Weekly*, 29 June 1970.

NOTES TO CHAPTER 4, pp. 49–56

1 Quoted from A. F. Kleinberger, *Society, Schools and Progress in Israel*, p. 176. Pergamon: Oxford, 1969.
2 The latest figures available when this was written (those for 1968–9) showed percentages stabilized at 65 per cent in State schools, 28 per cent in Religious State, 6–7 per cent in 'recognized' (i.e. Agudat Israel) schools.

NOTES TO CHAPTER 5, pp. 57–71

1 I. Domb, *Transformations*. Published by the author with an introduction by E. Marmorstein: London, 1958.
2 Quoted by E. Marmorstein, *Heaven at Bay*. OUP: London, 1969.
3 *Ibid.*
4 *Ibid.*
5 *Ibid.*
6 Dr Harold Fisch in correspondence with the author, quoted by permission.
7 Simha Friedman, 'The extension of the scope of halacha', in *The Religious Kibbutz Movement*. World Zionist Organisation: Jerusalem, 1957.
8 Tsuriel Admanit, 'On the religious significance of the community', *ibid.*
9 Eliezer Goldman, *Religious Issues in Israel's Political Life*. World Zionist Organisation: Jerusalem, 1964.
10 Harold Fisch, 'Faith in Israel', in *Commentary*. February 1969.
11 Harold Fisch in correspondence with the author, quoted by permission.
12 Professor Zvi Werblowsky, in a stencilled address 'Israel: the People and the Land', 1967. This address summarizes a longer paper published in French, in J.-P. Sartre's journal *Les Temps Modernes*, no. 253 *bis*, 1967.
13 Quoted by Jack J. Cohen in *Petahim*, English trans., June 1968.
14 Privately to the author.

NOTES TO CHAPTER 6, pp. 72–89

1 I. Domb, *Transformations*. Published by the author with an introduction by E. Marmorstein: London, 1958.
2 *Soldiers' Talk*, later translated as *The Seventh Day*, ed. Henry Near. André Deutsch: London, 1970.
3 *Bein Zeirim* (*Among Young People*), edited and published by members of the Kibbutz Movements and Am Oved, Tel Aviv, 1969.

4 *The Seventh Day*, p. 161.
5 This is true only metaphorically if at all. Zionist occupation was by freely negotiated purchase, and the Arab population grew during the course of it.

NOTES TO CHAPTER 7, pp. 93-199

1 J. W. Parkes, *End of an Exile*. Vallentine, Mitchell & Co. Ltd: London, 1954.
2 The reader will bear in mind the many co-owners, small business men and small proprietors on the land who are not part of the denominator of this fraction.
3 In 1968 and 1969 there were 71,000 immigrants, 40,000 from Western countries. Of the total, about a third were classed as 'professionals' (i.e. on a level normally requiring an academic degree) compared with one in seven of the Israeli population.

NOTES TO CHAPTER 8, pp. 101-14

1 Yitzhak Rabin, address to the Hebrew University, 28 June 1967. Magnes Press: Jerusalem.
2 Asher Walfish in *Israel: Towards a New Society*. Labour Zionist Movement: Tel Aviv, 1969.
3 Yehuda Amir, 'The effectiveness of the Kibbutz-Born Soldier in the Israel Defence Forces', *Human Relations*, Vol. 22, No. 4.

NOTES TO CHAPTER 9, pp. 115-19

1 A. F. Kleinberger, *Society, Schools and Progress in Israel*, pp. 297-307. Pergamon: Oxford, 1969.

NOTES TO CHAPTER 11, pp. 127-38

1 Dr Saul Esh, of the Institute of Contemporary Jewry in the Hebrew University, Jerusalem, at a London conference on 'Jewish Life in Modern Britain'. Papers and proceedings published under that title, eds Julius Gould and Saul Esh. Routledge & Kegan Paul: London, 1964.
2 *Ibid.*, paper on education by I. Fishman and H. Levy. The statement seems exaggerated.
3 Ernest Krausz, *Leeds Jewry*. Heffer: Cambridge, 1963.
4 Henry Near, 'Zionism and Jewish Culture', in *The Jews and the National Question*. Ichud Habonim: Tel Aviv, 1968.
5 'Jewish Education – For What?' in *American Jewish Year Book*, New York and Philadelphia, 1969.
6 Charles Liebman, 'The Role of Israel in the Ideology of American Jewry', *Dispersion and Unity*. World Zionist Organisation: Jerusalem, 1970.
7 See the account by Geoffrey Wigoder in the *Jerusalem Post*, 3 March 1970.

NOTES TO CHAPTER 12, pp. 141–8

1 Seventeenth-century codification of halachic rules and practice, still regarded as authoritative.
2 The Baal Shem Tov, Master of the Holy Name, the founder of Hasidism.
3 & 4 Leaders of the German Enlightenment, holding widely different views.
5 S. Dubnow, *Nationalism and History*, ed. Koppal S. Pinson. Jewish Publication Society of America: Philadelphia, 1950.
6 Leon Roth, *Judaism: A Portrait*, p. 15. Faber: London, 1960.
7 There is in Northern Ireland a limited exception which, seen in its full national context, proves the rule.
8 D. Ben-Gurion, *Ben-Gurion Looks Back*, pp. 221–2. Weidenfeld & Nicolson: London, 1969.

NOTES TO CHAPTER 13, pp. 149–164

1 From Doris Peel, 'Up to Jerusalem', *Christian Science Monitor*, 23 October 1969. Copyright, the Christian Science Publishing Society, all rights reserved. Quoted by permission.
2 Eliezer Schweid, 'On Being a Jew', reprinted in *In the Dispersion: 1968*. Jewish Agency Jerusalem, 1968.
3 *Prozdor* (English trans.), No. 6–7, September 1963.
4 Leon Roth, *Judaism: A Portrait*, p. 130. Faber: London, 1960.
5 *Ibid.*, p. 134.
6 *Petahim* (English trans.), No. 4, June 1968.
7 Fisch letters.
8 *NEB*, Habakkuk, ii, 3.
9 J. L. Talmon, 'Israel among the Nations', reprinted in *Confrontation*, pp. 15, 18. World Zionist Organisation: Jerusalem, 1970.
10 Herbert Weiner, *The Wild Goats of Ein Gedi*, pp. 171–2. Doubleday: New York, 1961.
11 Ernst Simon, 'Judaism: A Source of Culture', *Euros*. Paul Brand N.V., Hilversum.
12 Gershom Scholem, *Jewish Mysticism*. Schocken: New York, 1941–67.
13 Matthew, xxii, 36–40.
14 See Appendix, Note 7.
15 G. F. Moore, *Judaism in the First Centuries of the Christian Era*, Vol. I, p. 377. OUP: London, 1927. The passage, based on Berakot 34b, is worth reproducing. It refers to Rabbi Hanina ben Dosa. 'By his prayers a son of his master Johanan ben Zakkai was healed of a grave illness. Again, when a son of Gamaliel II was very ill, the father sent two of his disciples to Hanina ben Dosa that he might beseech God's mercy upon his son. Hanina at once went up to the chamber on the roof and prayed for him; when he came down he said to the messenger, Go, for the fever has left him. They asked, are you a prophet? He replied, I am neither a prophet nor the son of a prophet but I have learned that if I have freedom in prayer I know that it is accepted; if not, I know that it is rejected. They noted down in writing the hour at which he said this, and when they arrived at Gamaliel's house and reported

the matter, he said: By the divine service! At that exact hour, no more and no less, the fever left him and he asked for a drink of water!' Cf. John, v, 46–53.

16 S. H. Bergman, *Faith and Reason*. Schocken: New York, 1963.

NOTES TO APPENDIX, pp. 167–75

1 Charles Guignebert, *The Jewish World in the Time of Jesus*, trans. S. H. Hooke. Kegan Paul: London, 1939.
2 Joseph Klausner, *Jesus of Nazareth*. Allen & Unwin: London, 1927.
3 *Jerusalem Post Weekly*, 31 August 1970.
4 Quoted in Edmund Wilson, *The Dead Sea Scrolls 1947–1969*. W. H. Allen: London, 1969.
5 David Flusser, 'A New Sensitivity in Judaism and the Christian Message', *Harvard Theological Review*, No. 61, 1968.
6 David Flusser, 'Jesus in the Context of History', in *The Crucible of Christianity*, ed. Arnold Toynbee. Thames and Hudson: London, 1969.
7 David Flusser, 'Healing through the Laying-on of Hands in a Dead Sea Scroll', *Israel Exploration Journal*, Vol. 7, No. 2, 1957.

Index